GUUS HIDDINK

GOING DUTCH

GUUS HIDDINK

GOING DUTCH

MAARTEN MEIJER

RANDOM HOUSE AUSTRALIA

Photographic credits: while every effort has been made to contact all copyright holders, the publishers will be glad to make good in future editions any errors or omissions brought to their attention.

Random House Australia Pty Ltd
20 Alfred Street, Milsons Point, NSW 2061
http://www.randomhouse.com.au

Sydney New York Toronto
London Auckland Johannesburg

First published by Random House Australia 2006

National Library of Australia
Cataloguing-in-Publication Entry

Meijer, Maarten.
Guus Hiddink: Going Dutch.

ISBN 978 174166 530 7.
ISBN 1 74166 530 2.

1. Hiddink, Guus, 1946–. 2. Soccer players – Netherlands – Biography. 3. Soccer coaches – Netherlands – Biography.
I. Title.

796.334092

Cover photo courtesy of Getty Images/Dean Mouhtaropoulos
Cover design by Blue Cork design
Back cover photographs © Kim Kyung Hoon/Reuters/
Picture Media (top right), © PSV-Eindhoven (centre),
© Joongang (bottom right)
Typeset by Midland Typesetters, Australia
Printed and bound by Griffin Press, Netley, South Australia

10 9 8 7 6 5 4 3 2 1

CONTENTS

PROLOGUE

MEETING HIDDINK

At ten minutes to six Guus Hiddink strides into the lobby of the Seoul Grand Hyatt Hotel, with his shirt collar unbuttoned and tie in hand. We were supposed to meet at 5.30, but you don't mind a man in the global fast lane running a bit late. He apologises. '*Ik ben zo druk als een klein baasje*,' he says, which literally means 'I am as busy as a small company boss'. That is a nice Dutch understatement. Boss, yes, but hardly a 'small' company.

Because we are compatriots we speak Dutch, our common mother tongue. My teenage daughter, Renee, who was eager to come along to get a close look at the great man – and for the occasion is even sporting a T-shirt advertising Holland – does not speak the language. English is our domestic lingua franca. 'What *do* you speak?' Hiddink asks her in English – fluently, but laced with those heavy and articulate consonants the Dutch don't easily shed. 'English, Korean and Russian,' she answers. Afterwards, she manages to get her picture taken with him – which will make her an instant celebrity at the Korean school where she studies. After all, *everybody* would love to meet *Hi-ding-ku*. During Renee's photo opportunity he has to shoo off a few obstinate football tourists who wave cameras at him and want equal treatment.

So, why am *I* meeting him? To get a personal impression of this tall and relatively good-looking fellow who seems to be causing such a stir wherever he goes. And to find out why he gets the job done where others fail. Can something be learned from his management and leadership style that might have applications beyond the sports world, as some hopeful business school operators and starry-eyed social and political reformers insist? In the court of popular opinion, the well-spring of wisdom that is Hiddink occasionally seems limitless. After the pandemonium of World Cup 2002, a well-known Korean university launched a course in 'Dutch leadership'. Guru Hiddink, so went the theory, could do no wrong. During his time in Korea, no less than 25 volumes, written in Korean and dealing with the *Hiddink phenomenon*, were written.

Back home in the Netherlands, I mine football club archives, wading through piles of dull football statistics from yesteryear until happening upon some gems of rare biographical beauty. I conduct numerous personal interviews with people who know or have known Hiddink as friend, colleague or teacher. I go to towns where he once lived or worked to meet friendly neighbours and former classmates, all eager to talk. When someone rises to fame, everyone suddenly becomes an authority on the subject and it takes some sorting of the wheat from the chaff. But those who are or were close to him are generous with their time, stories and pictures. The anecdotes they tell me and the views they share have given this book its colour and soul. This seems to be the place to acknowledge these contributions, without which this biography would have been impossible. I also visit Hiddink's hometown and watch some of the World Cup 2002 matches with his relatives and acquaintances, most notably his aged parents. It is a pleasure and privilege to meet and speak with these common and yet extraordinary people.

This book is a portrayal of Hiddink's life, from his boyhood in the rural Netherlands to his latest adventure in Australia. It follows him through school, football trainings, his job as a teacher, his career as a professional football player to his current state as a world-class coaching superstar.

An enormous amount has been said and written about the mysterious man from the country of windmills and tulips. Yet, despite the sheer volume of publications and broadcasts, the picture of Hiddink, the man, has not necessarily become much clearer. On the contrary, news reports have added to the confusion through their ambiguity and contradictions. The sports media, maybe more than any other, is expert at churning out nonsense in quantity. As a man accustomed to being in the limelight, Hiddink accepts some of this as the inevitable by-product of football fame. But during our talk he does not hide his irritation at the half-truths and *kolder* 'balderdash' that is spread about him.

Who really *is* Hiddink?

When you meet him, you are immediately struck by his vigour and energy. There is no shortage of willpower and no lack of self-confidence. He's a man who knows what he wants. He knows where he is going. His height of around 1.8 metres and the fact that he manages to keep relatively fit for his 59 years, contribute to this image of strength. He is obviously a person of keen intelligence but not necessarily of the academic type. He possesses what people in New York, my wife's hometown, would call 'street smarts' – practical, applicable wisdom. He combines that, quite naturally, with a certain reserve and dignified sophistication. However, with all of this present, there is still space for some warm humanity, kindness and tolerance – 'charisma' the media have called it, and in this instance they are right.

I did not want to show up empty-handed so I give Hiddink the book I have brought along as a present: a

40-odd-year retrospective of a Dutch football club he once played for. When I was in the Netherlands, a week earlier, I interviewed a man who was the assistant coach during Hiddink's time. He was clearly proud of the publication and wanted Hiddink to have a copy. Hiddink leafs through the book and looks at pictures of old pals with undisguised, almost boyish delight. He has his reading-glasses perched on his nose, which gives him a distinguished, almost scholarly look. He keeps saying, softly, as if to himself: *Dit vind ik reuze leuk* and *hardstikke mooi* – 'I enjoy this tremendously', 'really beautiful'.

This book is not intended as the final word on Hiddink. It is a sympathetic portrayal written by a compatriot, a fellow Dutchman. I hope this book will shed some natural light on an intriguing and inspiring human being, working in a public environment that commonly generates more heat than light. Australians have landed a big fish in Hiddink and the Socceroos may well go farther than the naysayers – domestic or foreign – seem to suggest.

PART I

THE EARLY YEARS

VARSSEVELD

When you drive from west to east in Holland, or the Netherlands as the country is properly called, you leave the large cities behind and enter the open countryside. Buildings are replaced with lush green meadows, the famed black-and-white dairy cattle are omnipresent, and the pungent smell of cow manure fills your nostrils. The whole country is flat, with no mountain or hillock to break the monotonous straight line of the horizon. This is a great place for riding bicycles, something that almost every Dutchman or Dutchwoman does daily. In fact, there are more bicycles in the Netherlands than there are cars, and separate bicycle paths are a standard fixture, running parallel to roads for motorised traffic, even alongside rural highways.

The freeway that leads all the way from the capital, Amsterdam, to the eastern province comes to a sudden stop in Varsseveld, as if to emphasise that you have arrived at your destination. This is the hometown of Guus Hiddink. It is a small place, with less than 6000 inhabitants, very similar to many others in the rural Netherlands. Its main claim to fame is that it is a 'centre of equine events', as a tourist brochure points out without further elaboration. Yet, the town is so out of the way that it does not feature a hotel. After all, who would want to stay in the sticks of Gelderland, as the largest of the eleven provinces is called. That was, of course, before Hiddink put the place on the map.

The streets are mostly named after members of the royal family – citizens in the countryside are fonder of the monarchy than the western city dwellers are – or birds, cereals and even dairy products. This is farming country. In the central square is the Dutch Reformed Church. The foundations of the building are nearly a thousand years old and the original clock tower dates from the 1300s. The church has been restored and partially rebuilt several times. It is still by far the highest building in the town, as it has been for centuries. Judging by the town's main architectural landmark, God still has a say in things here. The bell in the tower faithfully strikes the hours; otherwise, the town is mostly quiet.

This area of the Netherlands is known as the *Achter-*

hoek or 'the back corner', because, seen from the better known and more prosperous west, it really is a sort of backyard of the country. Urbane city-dwellers think of the area as a kind of geographical appendix to 'where it's happening'. Yet people are proud of their land and their customs here. Sometimes they make fun of the cocky west-erners in a good-natured way. Hiddink's village is close to the border and people speak their Dutch with a distinct accent that shows some Germanic influence, although you had better not say so out loud because in their hearts most Dutch people still think they are somewhat superior to their old World War II enemies, the Germans.

Unlike people in the so-called big cities, like Amster-dam, Rotterdam and Den Haag (The Hague), folks here are not in a hurry and have time for each other. They get off their bicycles to have a little chat when they run into someone they know, and, unlike people in western cities, they are not suspicious of strangers but are kind and helpful. But they are not pushovers; they are strong-willed, some would say stubborn. If there is a downside to living in such a small community, it might be that it is hard to keep secrets here. Apparently, everybody knows pretty much everything about everybody else. Ask them about Hiddink and they will tell you: 'Guus? Yes, of course I know him', as if this is really nothing special. But everyone respects him as a person of integrity and is proud of his accomplishments.

Actually, there are quite a few 'Hiddinks' in this town, but many of them are no immediate relatives of Guus.

It's a common name in this part of the country. Hiddinks have lived here for centuries, and their legacy can be seen in the presence of a Hiddink dike, Hiddink bridge and Hiddink forest. Once upon a time, there was also a *Hiddink huus* ('house' in the Achterhoek dialect), the former café of Guus' grandfather, which unfortunately has a different use now and has been remodelled beyond recognition. Guus' direct ancestors were probably landed farmers who lived in and around the Varsseveld area from circa 1800. Staying put has shaped the family character and has been a source of individual and familial stability.

You notice many other names with the same ending on store signs, *Wessink*, *Hesselink*, *Fokkink*, *Geerdink*. When asked, locals explain that the ending –ink means 'son of'. *Hiddink*, then, would mean 'son of Hidde'. The name *Hidde*, in turn, is a shortened version of the Germanic form *Hild*, which means 'battle'. The family name *Hiddink* should be interpreted as something like 'son of a warrior'. *Guus* is the shortened version of *Gustav*, which comes from the Slavic name *Gostislav*. *Gosti* means 'stranger', and *slav* 'praise'. In summary, the meaning of *Guus Hiddink* would be something akin to: 'the praiseworthy stranger, son of a warrior'. There is little doubt that Hiddink himself would smile at such a convoluted translation. He wouldn't be interested in such academic excursions.

Now, on to the hard part – at least for the non-Dutch: how to pronounce his name. 'Hiddink' is pretty straightforward, but 'Guus' is a different story altogether. No, it is not 'Gus', and definitely not 'Goose'. The precise vowel sound is non-existent in the English language. The 'uu' is similar to the way the 'u' in DuPont (like the well-known maker of resins and polyesters) is pronounced by English speakers. The 'g' is worse. It is a rasping, guttural kind of sound, like a person with a bad cold clearing his throat. A speech therapist once told me that speaking Dutch is distinctly unhealthy for the vocal cords. If this indeed is true, then the northern Dutch are in graver danger of contracting maladies than those in the south because they rasp more heavily. Just keep it simple and don't even try . . . And don't worry, because Hiddink sympathises with the frustrations of his foreign supporters and does not really mind being called Gus or something similar.

PARENTS

Guus was born on 8 November 1946, as the third son of Gerrit and Jo Hiddink. Gerrit, who was a teacher all his life, worked in an even smaller neighbouring village until the family moved to Varsseveld in 1949. Locally, he is known as *meester Hiddink* 'master Hiddink', because for decades he taught at the local public elementary school, and from 1955 until his retirement in 1980, was its principal or 'headmaster', as it was called in the old days. He taught the school's senior class, and many boys and girls in town were under his care at one time or another. Guus was one of his pupils and, perhaps out of concern that his classmates might closely watch whether the headmaster's son received any preferential treatment, Gerrit Hiddink was very strict with his offspring.

Frits Kleinnibbelink – another 'ink' – used to be assistant coach at Sportclub Varsseveld when Guus played for the amateur football club. He now owns a health spa on the Koningin Wilhelminalaan, Queen Wilhelmina Lane. Guus' parents live on the same street just 70 metres away from the fitness centre. Kleinnibbelink used to teach physical education at the school where Guus' father was in charge. In an interview, he gave the following description of the practical wisdom and modesty of Gerrit Hiddink.

> *When I was just 19 years old, I started working as a teacher at the school. Master Hiddink invited me into his office to discuss the selection of special sports events for the coming year, such as a football tournament, a baseball competition, or an athletics trial. He cautiously offered many suggestions to me, a very inexperienced teacher. The next day, at a meeting with the other teachers of the school, he asked me, 'Well, what do you think? What is best for us to organise?' Then I spoke and presented what we had discussed in private the previous day, eighty per cent of which really came from him. Then he proceeded to give me all the credit, as a very young teacher, for all*

> *the good ideas he had provided me with. As result, I really gained the respect and admiration of all the others in the group, who thought, 'Boy, that young guy really has his head screwed on right!'*

Gerrit Hiddink is calm and down-to-earth, or *nuchter*, as the Dutch call it. This literally means to be 'sober'. But the implication for Dutchmen is that a person does not get carried away in the excitement and the emotions of the moment but rather rationally and deliberately considers the situation. This is a trait greatly valued in the Netherlands, and master Hiddink is in full possession of it. He and his wife were present when locals and visitors such as myself watched the World Cup 2002 game between Korea and Spain in a café together. The atmosphere was tense and people were gasping every time the Spanish team came close to scoring.

Meanwhile, about ten camera crews from the Netherlands, Germany and Korea were swarming through the place, bothering the invited guests with all their questions and glaring spotlights, especially Hiddink's parents. But Gerrit Hiddink remained his unperturbed Dutch self and never lost his poise. For a person unaccustomed to media exposure, he dealt very well with the herd of reporters. In a way, he seemed to enjoy his newfound celebrity status – probably not because of any unfulfilled personal need for public attention but because the focus was on his son. And despite his modesty and unflinching propriety, parental pride shone through. Later, when Guus returned from his triumphs in Korea, his father shook his hand and said, in a wonderfully concise understatement, 'Well done, my boy. Do you want coffee?' And his mother buttered him a currant bun. At home the supercoach is still a child and is appreciated for who he is, not what he's achieved.

Yet Gerrit Hiddink is not detached and certainly not unfeeling, as Kleinnibbelink explains:

> *When the Dutch national team placed for the quarterfinals of the 1998 World Cup in France, Royal Dutch Football Federation (KNVB) coach Hiddink said to a journalist in an interview, 'Tonight, I will open a bottle of wine to celebrate.' Then I got a bottle of wine and brought it over to his father and said, 'If the federation coach may break a bottle of wine on the occasion, then "daddy federation coach" is entitled to it even more . . .' Then he became very emotional and started to cry.*

Gerrit Hiddink also has a good sense of humour. It is a kind of dry, ironic humour, typical of the older generation of educated Dutch – funny and at the same time instructive to the listener, and never at the expense of others. When he was questioned by an interviewer from the media pack, a slightly pushy Dutchman this time and one who, judging by his accent, definitely came from the western region of the country, he said, 'You know, we are Achterhoekers here. We are people from the eastern part of the country. And do you remember who came from the east? Wise men . . .' – referring to the Magi, the educated noblemen who visited the infant Christ in Bethlehem.

There is a very serious side to Guus' father as well. He was active in the Dutch 'underground', a movement that resisted the Nazis during World War II. The German invasion interrupted the tranquil life of the Hiddinks as it did for nearly all the Dutch. Gerrit was studying education in university at the time. He had to stop his studies and worked as a clerk at City Hall for the duration of the war. The Nazis had developed a draconian food rationing system, allegedly to ensure that the needs of all citizens were met in a time of ubiquitous shortages, but in reality intended to maintain detailed demographic statistics and tightly control the population. Though the foreign invaders were in charge of the social and economic infrastructure of the Netherlands, day to day operations were still run by the Dutch. Many went along with this, out of fear of brutal reprisals, while others used their position to undermine the enemy's objectives and regain freedom.

Gerrit Hiddink belonged to the latter group. His position allowed him to 'lose' food ration cards and help make sure they got to those in real need. The Resistance had various techniques to cover its tracks, occasionally making these disappearances look like robberies. When the Nazi persecution of Jews intensified, many urban families sought refuge in the countryside and, with the help of the Resistance, relocated from Jewish population centres such as Amsterdam to rural places like Varsseveld. Hiddink senior helped save numerous Jews from certain concentration camp deaths. He did so at great personal risk; the Germans routinely executed those who were found hiding or otherwise supporting Jews. In addition, he helped to smuggle downed Allied pilots to safety through France, Switzerland and Spain.

For his bravery, he later received a letter of appreciation from the Allied Forces commander-in-chief, General Eisenhower. The epistle was framed and graced the walls of the Hiddink residence for many years. The headmaster is much respected throughout the community for the sacrifices he made during the war. He was later recognised for his social and humanitarian contributions by the Dutch government and was made a *ridder in de orde van Oranje Nassau*. He was formally knighted by the Dutch queen.

Gerrit Hiddink was also an accomplished football player. He played until he turned forty-three in the first team of SC Varsseveld. By that time, young Guus was already so good himself that he was put in the first team as well, as its junior player. So the interesting situation came about that father and son played in the same team for some time. Gerrit was, like Guus, a midfielder and also had the crisp, strong left-footed shot that his son would later develop. In many ways, in character and in sports it was 'like father, like son'. Master Hiddink liked football so much that 'he probably only accepted teachers in his school who also played well', joked Gert-Jan Tuenter, a local café owner. Tuenter was also once a student of Gerrit Hiddink and is obviously fond of his old teacher.

Hiddink's father is now eighty-nine years old, but looks like someone in his late seventies. He is bright, alert and stays active. 'I still keep moving. Keep on walking, then you don't die,' he says. In fact, he is in such good shape that if for some reason a designated referee was unable to cover a football game for the local club, he would be willing to referee it himself.

Jo Hiddink, Guus' mother, is eighty-five but looks at least ten years younger. She is as healthy and active as her husband and comes to Kleinnibbelink's health centre seven days a week to swim. She has always had a strong sense of personal responsibility and an acute awareness of what ought to be done for those in need. She seemed to be a magnet, drawing people with questions to be answered and problems to be solved to the Hiddink residence. New arrivals to the community would seek her out, and Jo Hiddink readily would assist them with getting settled. When she was the school principal's wife she was particularly well situated to help with educational matters. She met with students' parents when they visited the school, and often took care of children after school hours when their parents weren't able to. Old family photographs still bear witness to the abundant presence of children in and around the Hiddink home – for outsiders it is hard to tell who was a permanent resident and who wasn't. Jo Hiddink never rejected anyone's plea for help.

The social content and moral substance of their father's and mother's lives were not lost on Guus and his brothers. Gerrit Hiddink's dedication to teaching and to sports, and Jo's devotion to charitable action appear to have directly inspired the career choices several of their sons made. Taken together, the boys' occupational involvement manifests their father's and mother's inclinations in a rather well-proportioned and evenly balanced manner. The three youngest sons are a physical education teacher, the manager of a sports centre, and a social welfare professional working with handicapped children, respectively. Guus seems to have straddled the line distinguishing his paternal and maternal impulses more than anyone else. For more than a decade he taught physical education to children with learning disabilities before finally settling on a career in professional football. Homo ludens with a social conscience.

Both of Guus' parents personify the proverb 'a healthy mind in a healthy body'. Together, Mr and Mrs Hiddink have successfully raised six sons. Together, they still regularly bicycle the fifteen kilometres to the neighbouring town of Doetinchem to visit their sons. They display stoic old world calm and modest self-confidence, qualities in plentiful supply in surviving members of the 'older generation' but harder to find among those younger, in an era of fast food, the internet, self-indulgence and family breakdown that has thoroughly affected Dutch society. They are socially sensitive people and even now make themselves available to the community around them. Who else, at such advanced age, would appear at 8.30 in the morning in a smoke-filled café in the central town square to watch a football game with a large, boisterous crowd and dozens of reporters buzzing around? They could have watched it at home. But they didn't. These are Guus Hiddink's parents and much can be learned about the now famous coach by understanding his father and mother.

BROTHERS

A standard government sign announces in neat white letters on a navy blue background that you are entering the town of Varsseveld. But, unlike any other Dutch municipality, the town has a Korean translation posted underneath, in the official colours. Among a little clutter of miscellaneous signage promoting local businesses, there is another sign of note, certainly for those seeking to understand the deeper sources of Guus Hiddink magic. This one encourages people to make use of the services of Hans Hiddink's advertising agency. In a way, it is the business card of the Hiddinks, and Hans is the unofficial spokesman of the family. That is quite natural because he is also the only one of the six sons who is still living in Varsseveld.

Hans' office is behind his house, so ordinarily it is not difficult to find him. This man is a fount of information, insight and inspiration. He is also extraordinarily patient and helpful. Even in the thick of things during World Cup 2002, with a constant flow of telephone calls and visits from media people wanting to know the secrets behind his brother's successes, he was welcoming and responsive. With his grey moustache, he showed a distinct resemblance to Guus when he had one. But recently Hans, maybe prompted by his younger brother's newly established shaving habits, has removed his also. Hans is three years older than Guus.

> *There are six boys in our family. No girls. You could say that there are two groups: the older three – Wim, myself and Guus – then a break of seven years, and then the younger three – Arnold, René and Karel. I am the only one who doesn't play football. I chose music instead.*

The age difference between these two 'groups' made the older boys tend to stick together and ignore the younger ones. Their parents kept up their hopes for a daughter but it was not to be. The boys were aware of their parents' desire and consequently teased their youngest brother by saying, 'You are a girl!'

In a family with so many sons, part of the responsibility for leading the way fell to the oldest, Wim, by default. He was an eager student and of all the Hiddink boys was the only one to pursue a purely academic path; he became an engineer. Gerrit Hiddink had his hands full governing unruly youths at his elementary school all day and would often come home exhausted, so it was Wim who continuously challenged his younger brothers, and Guus in particular, to take their studies more seriously. Brother number three could be characterised as a slightly reluctant student. Whether the exhortations of his elder brother had the intended effect is doubtful. After school, Guus spent considerably less time bent over his books than he did kicking a football.

Hans and Guus seemed to agree that this older brother of theirs was a bit of a 'stiff'. Wim had decided, shortly after he joined the navy, that he was going to get engaged in style. The venue was an elegant, traditional Dutch sailing vessel, and he required his younger brothers to appear in 'proper' attire. That, of course, added fuel to the fire of his younger siblings' rebellious tendencies. Hans retold with relish how he donned his everyday garb and even managed to dig up an old farmer's cap for the occasion. On location he found Guus similarly dressed. No prior communication and planning had been needed – just common 'understanding' of what was called for under the circumstances. Naturally, grins were exchanged between the two nonconformists.

A common love for music had Guus and Hans sometimes staying out until the wee hours in 'chicken coop discotheques' of their own making: a stereo and some lights in a shed behind a farm. Once, when they returned around 4 am, they heard the church bell strike the hour. They got the inspired idea to wrap the clapper in a towel so that they would not be awakened later when sleeping in. Guus, standing on Hans' shoulders, did the job well. Unfortunately, they were implicated by the towel, which was somehow identified by the minister. The boys thought it was pretty funny, but the humour of the episode was lost on their father, who sternly lectured them on developing some personal awareness of which rules could be broken and which could not. Their father's earnest appeal to their own moral sense made a sufficiently strong impression on the two delinquents to prevent them from getting into more serious trouble in the future.

Hans nurtured his fondness of music and plays the banjo well. He and his jazz band Hot and Sweet provided the live entertainment in the café before and after the broadcast of the successful Korea–Spain match. He enjoys telling people he appeared on national TV before his now famous brother did, when he and his band won first prize in a national jazz festival in the 1960s. He plays in a second, larger ensemble, The Spirit of St Louis. Over the years he has garnered a collection of no less than 14,000 jazz tracks, which he is happy to ship to anyone, anywhere in the world.

Guus' brother René played for the pro-league club that is nearest to Varsseveld, De Graafschap, just as Guus did, and later in Germany. He is still active as a football coach. Karel, the youngest brother, played for years for FC Groningen and at one point even in the Dutch national youth team. In the family a lot revolved around football.

It was Hans' initiative to watch Korea play on a big screen in the café. Even in that public place, the welcome was warm: free breakfast was provided for all who entered. Hans had invited the whole Hiddink clan but, other than his parents, only Arnold came. The others were a little apprehensive at the thought of an army of journalists being on hand. René confided to Hans that he was getting tired of spending hours each day answering questions from nosy reporters. That did not seem to bother Arnold. Although he is ten years younger than Hans, Arnold's hair is greying, but this makes this tall, handsome man somehow even more appealing. He has the same pleasant, charismatic presence that characterises all the Hiddinks and kindly responded to all media questions, no matter how silly.

When asked how he thought Guus would respond to all the excitement surrounding him in Korea, Arnold answered:

> *He will absorb it all with a smile and will take it in with equanimity. He won't lie awake over it at night or have bad dreams about it. He is a very calm man, who develops a certain plan with clear objectives. He is flexible enough to adapt himself when he encounters particular*

> *challenges, but he still remains true to his original vision and pursues his goal. In addition, he has perfect timing, somehow. He knows where to be at what time. He is in the right place at the right time.*

When pressed a bit on how they think fame and glory affects their brother, both Hans and Arnold insisted that Guus' staying *gewoon*, 'normal, ordinary, like everybody else' is not just a pose. He genuinely dislikes being treated as a celebrity coach. He is Guus; and his profession is football coach. Period. In the autumn of 2005, he made a trip back from Australia especially to attend a reunion of his elementary school class. He crooned a baritone version of 'Summertime', accompanied by Hans' band, but according to Hans there is some room for improvement in his vocal skills. Otherwise, he received no hero's welcome. He's just one of the gang.

The brothers' view seems to be corroborated by Guus' own words on the subject. In Korea, he explained that he was 'not interested in heroism. I just do my job, and I love my job'. When his star rose to unprecedented heights, Hiddink accessories became best-selling items. When he was told that Hiddink dolls were selling like hotcakes, he observed, 'I would like to see that doll one of these days. I suppose it's pretty ugly. But I do not think that idolising any individual is desirable. That also isn't in line with what football should be about.'

But Guus does naturally take charge of things – he's

been a trainer too long. Around the time of the school reunion, he organised a dinner at the PSV club restaurant for family and friends. 'He immediately started coaching. One group had to get to the kitchen to help the cook; another group had to take care of the drinks; and the third team had to trim the tables,' said Hans. A rare exception to this rule of considering himself a regular Joe was when U.S. Secretary of State Colin Powell wanted to visit. That did make an impression, and he was unabashedly proud.

Hans volunteers some detail on what he believes is another important aspect of Guus' successful approach. 'When an Achterhoeker is ill, he sometimes prefers seeing a vet to going to the doctor. Because at the doctor's you have to *talk*, but the vet just *sees* and *feels* what is wrong with you.' A farmer takes a look at his cows and knows what's wrong with them. That's similar to how Guus deals with his players. No endless discussions and psychologising, but taking a good hard look and sensing what is the matter with a person.

Despite the friendliness with which the brothers Hiddink meet even complete strangers and patiently answer their questions, there also is a certain reserve. There are matters that are not discussed in public. It is clear that they protect their brother from unwanted intrusions into his personal life and expect people to respect their family's privacy. This is another vital Dutch virtue and one that is particularly valued here in the Achterhoek.

YOUNG HIDDINK

Guus Hiddink always was a man for the outdoors, not an office desk. Whenever he was asked, as a child, what he would like to be when he grew up, he would answer '*stront boer*', which means quite literally, 'shit farmer'. That clearly isn't a glamorous occupation, and Hiddink may have answered this way partly to get rid of his meddlesome brothers. 'I want to become a shit farmer,' in other words, a farmer who raises animals and sells the manure as fertiliser. This is still one of the favourite family quotes from Hiddink's early period.

But it wasn't just a joke. Judging by Hiddink's own

words on the subject, the fascination with farming was real.

> *Varsseveld was a rural town. When I was a child, I grew up in the middle of farms. After school finished, I always hurried to the homestead of farmer Harterink, an acquaintance. He had cattle and horses. Even as a child, I knew how to milk cows and when I was twelve, I learned how to plough a field. I loved that, with two horses in front pulling the plough. Every child has his dreams, and mine was to become a farmer. That seemed just wonderful to me.*

He also loved to spend time at his maternal grandfather's blacksmith shop and learned from him how to shoe horses. Even now, he sometimes longs for the smell of the animals he grew so fond of in that place. *Opa* (grandfather) Jan-Willem Prinsen had his own business and built a small fortune selling tractors and other agricultural equipment. Back in the 1930s, he was one of the few people in the area who owned an automobile and must have cut quite a picture rolling down the red-brick streets of the rural Netherlands in his American-made horseless carriage.

Grandfather Prinsen was a powerful influence in the life of little Guus. He taught him how to interpret animal behaviour, and the lessons learned may have helped

Hiddink later to better understand human actions. The old man would regularly take him out hunting pheasant or hare. Eventually, Guus earned the privilege of carrying his own gun. His first experience permanently cured him of any ambition to stalk game. As Hiddink explained:

> *When I turned seventeen I got my own hunting licence. Yes, my first shot was a hit. In my mind I can still see that hare topple over. After that, I suddenly did not like hunting anymore. Driving out the animals for others, okay, but shooting them myself, no. Later, when I again was one of a hunting party, I just kept quiet and left the hares in peace, even though I did see them. And I kept the dogs on the leash . . .*

Apparently, Hiddink's grandfather even let him cut classes for the sake of these wilderness experiences – which created a conflict of interest with his son-in-law, who just so happened to be the school principal. The old man had several hunting dogs and some of these evidently suffered from some form of canine fear of water. He would command his grandson to lead the way by example, strip to his underwear and jump into the local creek in order to help the cowards overcome their apprehension. The eight- or nine-year-old Hiddink had to go through this harrowing routine regardless of the season. These boot camp experiences may have reinforced Hiddink's native willpower. In the process, he probably also inherited some of grandfather Prinsen's ideas about the efficacy of purposeful and strong leadership.

Not everything in Hiddink's youth was idyllic. He was a teenager growing up in the rebellious 1960s. He did not easily submit himself to authority and was inclined to provoke reactions from people. He ignored strict rules, simply because they were strict rules and because he thought he knew better. Authority was suspect by definition.

He got involved in some local youth gangs, though the crimes committed were relatively innocent by modern-day standards. Each group had its own territory and turf wars ensued when the boundary lines were trespassed. 'We also stole boats. There was a winding creek from Varsseveld to Aalten. We would go down there, pull a boat from its moorings and take it for a joy-ride.' Afterwards, the police would provide the appropriate accommodation.

> *Looking back it was maybe a little silly, but when you're young you think those things are a thrill. But then to sit in the police station later, especially being the son of the school's headmaster; that was really something. After all, the headmaster was one of the town's dignitaries, in the same league as the mayor and the minister.*

He doesn't really remember if he was punished for his misdeeds at home. If so, it probably wasn't too severe because it didn't make a lasting impression.

Two of the boys were the ringleaders – Guus and another boy, who derived his authority from the fact that their group's meeting 'hut' was on his father's farmland. They had a lot of fun, but there were tense moments as well. Sometimes they would go poaching. Not game, but fish. In that very same creek, they caught pike and carp by pulling a dragnet through it. Without a licence, of course. And they were big fish they caught there, up to half a metre in size. 'Pike stand still in the water. The greatest thing was to try to catch them with your hands. Once or twice, that worked.' It was easier with the net, though, and they would catch up to seven or eight pike at a time. Then they would roast and eat them at the home of one of their friends, whose father owned a flower shop and did not mind the smell of fried fish blending with the fragrance of his floral arrangements.

There are some more Hiddink confessions:

> *My oldest brother had a scooter and when he wasn't around I would take that thing from the shed and would race through the forests with it, to my heart's content. When I was sixteen I was given a moped, a Rap Rocky. Nobody in our town had a Puch [a popular German moped brand]. Boys from Den Haag rode on*

> *Puchs . . . In the Achterhoek it was a big thing if you just had a Kreidler, but back then they cost about a thousand guilders [the old pre-euro currency; the equivalent of approximately A$700, a lot of money in those days]. A friend of mine did have a Kreidler, and I was envious as heck. But my parents could not afford such things, having six children.*

Though Guus' interest in farming was eventually displaced by his fascination with sports, his love of a ride through the countryside remained. Even now, Hiddink has a motorcycle, a Harley-Davidson. An acquaintance explained that when Hiddink was responsible for the selection of the national team, he had to call all over Europe to gather the best Dutch players from various foreign clubs. Having spent all day on the phone he would have, as he himself put it, '*een houten kop*' 'a wooden head'. So he would jump on his bike to clear out his head, riding through the farmlands of the Achterhoek. Late in the evening he would suddenly show up, out of the blue, at his friend's home, for a cup of coffee. The conversation would easily run for an hour and would hardly ever touch on the subject of football. 'Farmer Hiddink' had now become 'coach Hiddink', but also a man of the world, who could easily converse on a wide range of topics. In one and the same human being, the cosmopolitan qualities of an educated, well-travelled world citizen dwell side by side with the desires of a boy drawn to the simple delights of the Dutch countryside.

EDUCATION

In his high school photographs, Guus Hiddink stands off to the side, in a far corner. Judging by the pictures, he preferred not to be the centre of attention. Yet, in some of those shots he is making faces at the camera, grinning, and obviously enjoying himself. This is the Hiddink that is always ready for a joke, a prank, some comic relief. And according to peer reports, he was quite popular with the girls. In another old black-and-white shot, Guus is pictured in his swimming trunks, with female company close by. His high school years coincided with the heydays of rock 'n' roll and Guus was certainly a fan. He was particularly fond of the Rolling

Stones. He had his hair gelled and styled like Elvis Presley. Actually, in some of his pictures he shows some resemblance to James Dean. According to brother Hans, Guus liked the movie *Rebel without a Cause*, but was not a real troublemaker.

After finishing his elementary education at his father's school, Hiddink attended the HBS, the Hogere Burger School, the 'higher civilian school', in Doetinchem. Like most other Dutch boys of that time he got around on bicycle, and he made the daily round trip of approximately 30 kilometres on his non-motorised two-wheeler. Every morning at seven, a group of about thirty children gathered at café De Kempe and made the trek to Doetinchem, rain or shine, over the small country roads of the Achterhoek. It was important to participate in this daily ritual because those who went by bus were considered 'sissies'.

The HBS was a fairly prestigious establishment. Students who completed their education at the institution were allowed to enter university. Thus, graduation from this type of high school provided some kind of assurance of a decent job in the future. But according to Hiddink's own admission, his HBS experience was not a success. He liked studying languages, but he didn't think much of maths. It was not that he lacked the intelligence, but the academic subjects simply did not interest him. He was too playful. Immediately after school he would go out to play football or spend time with the horses. After three years he was still only in second grade.

Then he switched schools and went to the MULO, a

vocational junior high school back home in Varsseveld. 'My parents didn't really know what to do with me. I didn't know either. The only thing I knew was that I wanted to leave home and wanted to experience something more than just the Achterhoek.' The outcome of an aptitude test was: 'Well-suited for a leadership role.' Hiddink thinks that was primarily because he conducted himself in a 'somewhat domineering manner'.

When he was seventeen, he became more definite about his life's direction and started attending the CIOS, the central institute for teachers of physical education. It was not easy to enter this school – of 2000 annual applicants only twenty were admitted. His school grades were only fair, so Hiddink must have made an impression on the admissions committee in some other way. This junior college was in Overveen, near Haarlem, a mid-size city just west of Amsterdam.

The course of studies lasted two and a half years. The first year covered sports theory, anatomy, sports psychology and a whole range of sports including swimming, baseball, basketball, boxing, karate and judo. In the second year, students were allowed to select majors. Guus obviously chose football and over the remaining year and a half learned about the theory of football, the various aspects of physical training and team management. Basketball and baseball were his minors. In the Haarlem of those days, baseball was a big thing and Hiddink regularly watched the games. In his second year, he also had to do an internship, which he did with

De Graafschap, the pro-league football club near his hometown that he later joined full-time.

The school was tough. The organisation was, according to Hiddink, 'rather militaristic'. The experience only intensified his desire for freedom and independence. 'They didn't just wake you up in an ordinary manner. No. Summer or winter, at 6.30 am sharp, all the windows were thrown open and everybody was shouted out of their beds.' Praying before meals in the school cafeteria was a reckless undertaking. 'Whoever closed his eyes lost his eggs in no time. Many boys lost their faith in that place.' Classes started at 7.30 am and lasted until 6 pm. Then there was a lot of homework to do. Unlike the Netherlands of today, there were classes on Saturdays as well, until 2 pm.

The distance between Haarlem and Varsseveld is approximately 200 kilometres, and Hiddink stayed in the boarding house during the week and went home only after the conclusion of his studies on Saturday. Usually short on money, he hitchhiked his way back east. After the football match in Varsseveld on Sunday, he had to quickly return to Haarlem. His mother usually gave him money for the train.

The CIOS did have certain benefits though. Sometimes the famous Dutch judoka, Anton Geesink, came to visit. He had defeated the Japanese at their own game and had won gold medals at the judo world championships in 1961, and the 1964 Olympics in Tokyo. The Japanese revere him as a hero to this day. Of course, all of the boys wanted to sit at his table in the dining room and see what the master had to say. That didn't last too long because this bear of a man piled the food up so high on his plate that nothing much was left in the communal bowl for others.

Another noteworthy connection Hiddink made was with fellow student Leo Beenhakker, who later became coach of the Amsterdam pro-league club Ajax, for many years considered the Netherlands' premier football club. Hiddink was nineteen when he graduated from the CIOS, cum laude.

Hiddink never stopped learning outside school. He expanded his knowledge of foreign languages – very useful in the international football circuit. Today he is fluent in English, Spanish, French, German and, obviously, his native Dutch. He also understands basic Italian. More importantly, he acquired a wealth of practical wisdom. He learned to read people rather than books; he learned to recognise people's strengths – courage, endurance, generosity – and work with them; he learned to recognise human vulnerabilities – laziness, prejudice, egoism – and work around them.

PART II

HIDDINK THE PLAYER

FOOTBALL

If the drive to play football is not genetically determined, perhaps it was Hiddink's father's enthusiasm for the sport that infected several of his sons. During World War II and in the years after, Gerrit Hiddink was a well-known football player in the Achterhoek. Hans Hiddink said that he was often referred to as 'the Stanley Matthews of Varsseveld'. (The legendary British 'Magician' was the first football star knighted by the British queen, making him 'Sir Stan'.) He always played for the local team, because in those days playing for the club of another town was simply not done and professional football did not yet exist.

Though several of the Hiddink boys loved football from an early age, Guus was in a class of his own. 'Football always played a central role in his life,' said Hans. 'He could use his feet with the same ability as ordinary people use their hands.' Little three-year-old Guus was already a devotee of the sport. His father explains: 'He started playing football when he was a small boy. He even practised in the hallway of our house!' Whenever he came home from school, he would go somewhere to play 'tennis-football' – kicking the ball off a wall, to fine-tune his shot – preferably, against the walls of the neighbours' house. 'If I or anybody else did that, we would get it. But not Guus! Even then his nickname was "Guus *Geluk*" (a reference to a proverbial Dutch "Gus Good Luck"). Mine was "Hans *Tweedehands*", "Hans Second-hand",' complains the older brother. Little Guusje (the Dutch often add the diminutive –je to create a term of endearment) was everybody's darling. 'A little charmer if ever there was one. And looking cute to boot.' When Guus became a little older, some of these practice sessions got out of control and he landed his football inside a neighbour's house, breaking a window en passant. Then he had to make a quick getaway.

In elementary school he and his friends started to play football in earnest. By virtue of being the best player, Hiddink was usually a team captain and got to pick the boys on his side. The clever youngster understood that all kids want to be instant heroes, which means they want to score goals – the only thing that really matters at that age. He also quickly realised that in a field full of hotshots seeking personal glory, the defence is left full of holes. So he would always select a few self-sacrificing souls who did not mind playing in defence.

Guus hated to lose. As a child, he would shed tears over an upset and retreat to his room or nature to digest a disappointment in quiet solitude. Sometimes it would take him days to recover his balance. This difficulty of coming to terms with games that went against him lasted until he was in his twenties. Such anguish is a thing of the distant past, and the mature Hiddink displays admirable self-discipline in public when things run counter to expectations, unlike some of his less sophisticated colleagues. He is gracious and sportsmanlike whether his side wins or loses. Pictures of a visibly moved Hiddink, compassionately embracing Portuguese superstar Figo after the Korea–Portugal World Cup 2002 victory, were circulated in the world media. Nevertheless, the same dogged determination to win has survived to this day.

When his elementary school team played against a competitor from another neighbourhood, he rejected weaker players because he didn't want to lose. It was tough medicine, but this survival of the fittest approach did bring good results and his team won most of the time. These types of tactics can still be seen in the trademark Hiddink insistence on recruiting new talent to create the right team composition and placement based strictly on performance – never mind the pecking order or public opinion.

He started playing with SC Varsseveld from an early age. By the time he was fourteen he was already playing in the first team. This was no surprise to many of the older connoisseurs of village football. They had had their eyes on the boy with the sharp kick for some time. Gerard Schuurman, another first team player and a later club president, said:

> *Once I saw Guus field a corner kick in the youth team. Whereas others could barely land the ball in front of the goal, he produced a clear and straight cross. Even then, his overview of the game was one of his strong points.*

Hiddink himself remembers little of his early performances. But he does remember receiving the announcement that he had been enlisted in the first team.

> *Back then that happened by mail. You received a typed notice at home, informing you of the fact that you were invited to be a part of the first team of Varsseveld and that you had to report at a certain time at café De Kempe. Then it said, 'During the upcoming game you will be positioned as . . .' In my case, the blanks were filled with neat handwriting saying 'left forward'.*

Later team planners had a better understanding of his inborn skills and relocated him to where he felt at home: the midfield.

In those days he was filled with admiration for many of the players of his new team, all of whom were older than he was. Often, the players on the opposing team appeared even more awe-inspiring. The main asset of one of the opponents they once faced was an enormous player named Gradus Kuiper, who, in Hiddink's estimate, wore a shoe size 12½. To make matters worse, this giant warned him not to get too close, or else . . . Hiddink still remembers that when he prepared to receive a pass from one of his team mates, this character kicked him into the air while the ball was still six metres away.

Frits Kleinnibbelink explained the unique qualities of a left-footed midfielder.

> *As a midfielder he had to be an architect and decide the lines of the game. Besides, left-legged players are somehow always special. When Guus saw my son, who is also left-footed, play football, he told me: 'Don't worry. You don't have to teach anything to a lefty. They figure things out by themselves.' Apparently, they are more creative and, in addition, can somehow curve their shots better. Guus could anticipate the development of an attack. He could pass the ball perfectly to an offensive player, putting him in a position to score.*

The seriousness of Hiddink's commitment to football did not prevent him from manifesting his native sense of humour. Once, when he was tackled rather hard, he fell flat on the field, which happened to be quite muddy at the time. His hands were covered with dirt. The opponent who had tackled him came up to him, apologising: 'Sorry that I put you down like that.' Hiddink then kindly held the young man's head with his hands and responded: 'Don't worry; it could have happened to me.' The gullible youngster did not immediately notice that, as a result of Hiddink's brotherly embrace, he now was wearing a full mud beard.

The mature Hiddink is undeterred and pursues the love of his life with undiminished zeal.

> *My hobbies are music and football. People wonder how my job could be my hobby as well, but that's just the way I am. I analyse video tapes of daily training sessions and make plans for the next program . . . Enjoy. Enjoy your work. When I say that, the Koreans make a long face. That means that they don't take me seriously. But if you love your work, you take it seriously and then you get good results. They think that enjoying something is the same thing as idling around. But truly enjoying something has a completely different meaning.*

DE GRAAFSCHAP

When Hiddink was still at school in Doetinchem as a teenager, he would often make a little detour on his bicycle past De Vijverberg, the stadium of De Graafschap, just to catch a glimpse of the stadium, large and impressive, and the field, lush and green. The club has, in one way or another, been a constant presence in Hiddink's life. After he finished his education in Overveen, he returned to the Achterhoek and became youth trainer at De Graafschap. At that time, he was younger than some of the boys he was training.

These days, with the advancement of professional football to greater levels of sophistication, European clubs scout for talent and enrol young naturals in football schools from the age of eight. When Hiddink set out on his career in pro-football, players still went through all the amateur stages before being enlisted on a professional basis. He bypassed this regular circuit and was unexpectedly launched as a professional player. Ad Zonderland, the head coach at the club, recognised both his skill and his itch to kick the ball around, and asked if he wanted to start playing with the first team. From 1967 to 1970, Hiddink worked with De Graafschap as an assistant coach and an attacking midfielder, an uncommon combination.

> *I had stopped playing with Varsseveld in my second year at the CIOS. When I started coaching at De Graafschap I realised that it was still much too early to throw in the towel. Besides, after some practice games with the first team, I discovered that I wasn't any worse than most of the team's players.*

As in Varsseveld, he got to play with people he had deeply admired and he again experienced the same trepidation as during his initiation in the first team of his hometown, although a little less this time. Together with a couple of other players, Hiddink lived in a house owned by the club in de Vondelstraat in Doetinchem. It was a bachelor household. Guus explains:

> *A household of three boys. Can you imagine what a mess that was? We would often cook in pots dirty with the crusts of the previous meal preparation. But we didn't go out on the town. I never sat in cafés until deep in the night then.*

Despite the chaos, it was a great time for Hiddink.

It was also the start of Hiddink's football successes. When he arrived, the club was still listed in the second league of Dutch pro-football. A promotion to the first league followed soon afterwards. He was an old-fashioned 'number ten', left midfielder, in the tradition of the famous Dutch player Willem van Hanegem. He had a powerful left leg with which he could field an accurate shot over a distance of 40 metres and was liberal with long cross passes, particularly as he did not like to run. He was also stubborn, a feature common to quite a few Achterhoekers, and one which brother Hans readily recognises in his younger sibling. 'Once he has a certain idea in his head, it is almost impossible to change his mind.' These particular characteristics became more evident as he flourished at De Graafschap.

Kleinnibbelink, who got his trainer's licence shortly after Hiddink did, reappeared at De Graafschap and became Zonderland's assistant in 1972. He had many stories to tell of those early days.

> *Guus was very naughty. When we went out to play against Heerenveen [a club from a*

> *provincial town in the northern Netherlands], they gave us krielaardappeltjes (tiny round potatoes) in a large bowl for dinner. Guus picked up the bowl and pretended that he was putting everything on his own plate. Then he asked, with a sideways glance, 'Or do you guys want to have some, too?' At another time, on our way to practice, we were carrying a net full of balls. He walked in front of us. Suddenly he looked over his shoulder and ducked really fast as if to avoid an oncoming ball. Everyone bent down quickly in response. Of course, nothing was coming. Henk Overvoor, one of the players, was a buddy of Guus' who happened to be very afraid of cows. Of course, Guus would kick a ball intentionally out of the training grounds into the meadows where the cattle were grazing. And then he would make Henk get the ball . . .*

In addition to his club activities, Hiddink started attending evening classes at the Academy of Physical Education in Doetinchem to get his physical education teacher's licence. After two years, graduates from the college were qualified to teach at high school and university levels. This work–school regimen kept him on his toes: he taught kids in the morning, coached the pro-team in the afternoon, and studied three or four nights a week. Meanwhile, he lived pretty much hand-to-mouth.

HOMING PIGEON

Hiddink unites two contradictory traits: a thirst for adventure and a loyalty to tried relationships. These two qualities have, respectively, compelled him to wander over the world, engaging himself in one new football enterprise after another, and brought him back home to people and places dear to him, time and again. This makes life more complicated, in a way, because the attachments are increasing in number. Years after his debut at De Graafschap, Hiddink himself put it quite clearly, when he was asked whether he would ever consider returning to De Vijverberg as coach:

> *I can't say if I would, even though a large part of my heart is in that place. But I also still enjoy visiting Valencia. And recently, I was invited to the centennial of Real Madrid by Jorge Valdano (Sporting Director of the Club). I had to say no to that because I had obligations in Korea. Also, I still have a lot of contacts with PSV.*

Still, the Achterhoek is special to him because his roots are there. And Doetinchem and De Graafschap, in particular, are close to him because this is where he got his first real break as a semi-pro player. Hence, it is no surprise that he returned to this eastern Dutch football centre not just once but twice – in 1972 and in 1981. Despite all his travels throughout the world he maintained his permanent residence in the Doetinchem area for decades. 'I feel free there. I know the people. I meet this person and then that person, and I enjoy it. I feel myself a little like a homing pigeon: I roam all over the world, but this is my home base.' Of all the players who ever wore De Graafschap colours, Hiddink is, without a doubt, still one of the most popular. As a matter of fact, he has been referred to as 'the De Graafschapper of the century'.

In 1970, PSV-Eindhoven (Philips Sport Vereniging, 'Philips Sports Association') paid about A$300,000 for his transfer from De Graafschap. This was his first personal brush with a club he eventually would spend many years at, and it wasn't a happy encounter. Part of the problem was that the organisation was overstocked on midfielders, some of them more experienced than Hiddink. At least, the coach apparently thought so. Thus Hiddink would spend most of his time sitting on the bench. He played, or sat out, close to thirty games at the club but scored only once – frustrating for a man who netted twenty-two goals in one season at his previous club.

He was invited back to De Graafschap. Though he was rather eager to move, he had some difficulty with the way the transfer was accomplished. In those days, the club was constantly short of money and was not in a position to buy their former playmaker back. This led to the, by now, famous action *Een tientje voor Guus*, 'Ten guilders for Guus'. Supporters could drop a ten guilder bill in a milk can. Thus, the required 40,000 guilders were collected (approximately A$30,000). This gave the 'prodigal son' a sense of indebtedness and a feeling that he must not fail.

> *Of course it was a source of pressure. Those people had given from their own limited resources, so now I had to do something for them in return. Under those circumstances I had only one solution and that was to give myself one hundred per cent. Pressure stimulates me.*

Hiddink smilingly tells anecdotes of how, even now, he meets people on the street who tell him, in the unique eastern dialect, 'You still owe me ten guilders!' He wasn't getting any younger and had lost some of his speed. A striker–midfielder doesn't just give passes but alternately joins the defence and the attack. He has to run all over the field, a physically challenging job. To compensate for his physical shortcomings, Hiddink worked on his passes. Because he was an experienced player he could see the big picture on the field well, and the coach assigned him to a 'free-style' position, which he used to translate the coach's strategy to the players on the field. The pressure evidently did work and got results. In 1973, for the first time in its history, De Graafschap was promoted to the *eredivisie*, the 'honor league', the top league of Dutch professional football.

Still, Hiddink does not allow his sense of loyalty to force him into strained relationships. He commits himself to people but makes sure he does so on terms he is comfortable with. When he speaks of 'pressure', this should be understood as causing an invigorating adrenaline rush, not nail-biting anxiety. The following comment, made some time after his 'subsidised' return to De Graafschap, serves as an illustration:

> *I cannot say of myself that I am indispensable. I just feel certain that I am in the right position. Maybe this sounds a little frightening to some, but I am not really anxious. If they found an equally qualified man for my spot, I really wouldn't mind. In the same way,*

I was genuinely happy when the boys of NEC won. [Nijmeegse Eendracht Combinatie, 'Nijmegen Unity Combination', one of De Graafschap's prime opponents during the 1974 season.] Martin Haar made a goal for them, and I sincerely congratulated him after the game. You wouldn't do a thing like that if you weren't certain of your place.

Hiddink's modesty is not a self-conscious exercise in humility but a natural result of his quiet self-confidence.

When things go wrong, you often have to take the blame. Personally, I don't really care about that. You have a certain job to do and you have to accept the implications. Also, I'm not the kind of person who says after a game spent on the bench: 'I wasn't playing and just look what happened!' I don't like that.

NO FOOTBALL

Hiddink maintains a clear separation between his public persona and his private life, his football career and relations with family and friends. Though this is not uncommon for people with a certain celebrity status, Hiddink preserves the division with particular ardour. His private life is everything that does not deal with football. People who show insensitivity to his reluctance to talk about football at small gatherings may get the cold shoulder. Vice versa, journalists and other busybodies who stick their noses into his private affairs get nowhere. Coen Poulus, who played in De Graafschap's first team with Hiddink, explains:

> *Don't prod into his private life. If you do, you may get some blunt remark in return. He definitely emanates a certain dignity, so much so, that you really don't ask any more after a rebuff like that . . . He has a lot of authority. He gradually developed that.*

Poulus typifies him as a *gezelligheidsdier* – literally something like a 'cosiness animal' or 'sociability creature' – someone who thoroughly enjoys the company of other people. Frequently, after a game finished around 4 pm, members of De Graafschap's first team would spend the rest of their day together at one of the players' homes, together with wives and girlfriends, often until ten at night. It was a close-knit team. 'For each other, with each other,' says Poulus. It was the human dimension that mattered at those gatherings, not the professional one.

At birthdays and parties Hiddink always was, and still is, a welcome guest.

> *He has enough intelligence and perspective to see the relative importance of the whole [football] enterprise. Of course, it has its beautiful moments, but the successes can also finish all of a sudden. So he thinks, 'Let me enjoy myself along the way.' That positively affects his relationships. Guus is a very sociable person. But even then, suddenly, he can separate himself from a group by putting on a mask and*

> *look for peace by distancing himself. Or sometimes he really lets himself go at parties, shouts it out, on top of the table. Then I think, 'Man, you really are under so much pressure.' Occasionally, he just has to blow off steam, let it all out. Next moment, the storm is past. In Doetinchem people understand and accept this.*

Oud De Graafschap (Old De Graafschap) is a kind of alumni association of the club. Sometimes, the old-timers get together for a benefit game on occasion of the anniversary of some social or sports organisation that is short of money. Whenever Hiddink is in the country and he is called about one of these events, he makes an effort to attend. As Poulus says: 'He doesn't promise anything. But if he can, he just shows up. If he has to, he will cancel some TV interview for it.' He does not come for the football but purely for *gezelligheid* cosiness.

Socially, Hiddink is an easy and uncomplicated person. He prefers to be surrounded by people he knows. All year long he works under pressure, travelling the world. Then, when he has some vacation time, he wants some peace, silence and simplicity. So he turns up in his beloved Terschelling, a picturesque, quiet island off the northern Dutch coast. Or he rides his motorcycle in the Achterhoek and plays a game of golf or tennis. Poulus provides some perspective:

> *My daughter lives abroad and sometimes comes over for a visit with her Spanish husband. Then*

> *he sees Hiddink sitting in a local café and asks: 'Is that possible here in the Netherlands? That's Hiddink!' In Spain a famous coach would not be able to sit in a café like that, without drawing a crowd. But should we all of a sudden start to treat him differently here, now that he is well known? People would not accept that, and he would not want it himself.*

The Hiddink marriage has been fodder for the Dutch paparazzi. In reality, not much is known about Hiddink's family, exactly because of the well-cultivated separation between the work and home spheres, which, in later years, has been not only social, but also geographical. As Hiddink's sons were growing older, the family increasingly stayed in the Netherlands, while the coach roamed the earth. So little is publicly known about Mrs Hiddink that one Dutch journalist wrote in an article about her, 'Iene Hiddink exists', as if this were some startling new discovery.

In *Top Club PSV*, a book from 1970, Hiddink revealed something about the mysterious marriage, for the first and last time: 'I married Iene Beumkes, on 18 August 1969. How I met my wife will remain a secret. That is nobody's business.' Whatever else the quiet Dutchman said in public about his life partner was released incidentally, usually in connection with his profession. Once he said:

> *The life of a coach is a decadent existence and it easily spoils you. Very quickly you start snapping your fingers at people. So it is always good when Iene is around. She tells me: 'Hello, I don't wear a shirt number, mind you! Act normally, Guus.'*

Hiddink has definite ideas about what a woman should be like. 'Equal job – equal payment, that's fair. But please let women stay feminine.' It seems that Iene has obliged. People who have met her were struck by her womanly grace and style.

Unfortunately, although the marriage has lasted for thirty years, it seems to have come to an end. According to one Doetinchem acquaintance, 'We just can't figure it out. His attitude is something like, "I still love you, but . . ." He still seems to be very fond of her. We just don't understand.' Guus and Iene are not formally divorced. 'Much too expensive,' interprets Hans. But they worked out an arrangement in which she gets a comfortable allowance. Hiddink's two sons seem to be faring well. His youngest, Mark, born in 1972, owns a 'videotheque' named 'Las Vegas' in Doetinchem and plays decent football. For the time being, his elder brother Michel, born in 1969, assists in the store. He does not play.

Kees Ploegsma, former general manager of PSV during the Hiddink days, provides some further background:

> *All of them [players and coaches alike] are career makers. A little ambitious, a little vain. Besides, if they are successful, they are able to become financially independent in a short time. But that comes at a price. They've got a kind of 'football virus' that compels them to accept new challenges, over and over again. Privately it has its consequences, in nine out of ten cases.*

Currently, Hiddink has a girlfriend, Elizabeth, of African descent. She is an educated person and was working on her Master of Arts degree while accompanying Hiddink to the Far East. A thinking woman; a thinking man's woman. Apparently her skills in the area of conflict resolution came in handy during the occasionally bruising negotiations with the power-brokers of the Korean football world. She is a socially sensitive person and encouraged Hiddink to create a charitable foundation to support Korean adoption agencies. (In Korea single mothers are not covered by social welfare and thus often have no other option than to give their children up for adoption.)

Koreans tend to be direct about matters that are considered private in the west. They ask people about their age or marital status in first meetings without hesitation. Society is morally much more conservative than in the Netherlands, and on a few occasions Hiddink was confronted about his, by Korean standards, liberal liaison with Elizabeth. In the earlier stages of his Asian experience, when a reporter asked him who accompanied her in his absence, he reacted strongly: 'I feel like giving you a kick in the head.' But because of his very high-profile role and also because she was a steady presence at his side, he could not completely avoid the issue. Maybe he also gradually understood that Koreans feel that public figures ought to give some account of their personal doings to society, and that their curiosity, which would be interpreted as intrusiveness in the west, was not necessarily malevolent.

When asked why she often stayed at the same hotel as the team and regularly accompanied him to a training session or official gathering, Hiddink was more forthcoming: 'I am very hot-tempered. She calms me by standing next to me.' He went on to assure the inquisitive: 'Elizabeth will never be a distraction during the training of the team. She will not eat together with the team. She is not participating in the training. But where she goes and what she does is her own business.' Still, some awkward exchanges kept occurring. When he was asked at a press conference if he intended to marry her, Hiddink voiced unambiguous disapproval: 'Let go of the microphone and look for another job.'

Though Elizabeth is in the public eye more than her predecessor, Hiddink stays vigilant in protecting their privacy. Thus, his mixed relationship with the media continues. He shields her from interrogations as he did Iene. In this area, as in others, he is very consistent.

AMERICA

The years 1976–77 were important to Hiddink's development. At the time of his transfer from De Graafschap to NEC, he expressed the desire to work in the United States and ended up playing two summer competitions there. He said that the additional work was no burden to him: 'These were work-holidays for me. I was attracted by the adventure and could maintain my form well. As a consequence, I felt in much better shape during the preparation for the next [winter] season in the Netherlands.' There were no serious monetary issues involved. As a general rule Hiddink does not make his moves based on financial considerations but on the appeal of a new opportunity. In this case, his wish was simply to experience the American football scene. He started at the Washington Diplomats, which was, in his own evaluation, a pretty good club. As usual, he was a midfielder, the play-maker of the team. He was also the star player. He was challenged by American east coast humidity and in the process of adjusting to the climate shed three or four kilograms.

Next season, he transferred to the San Jose Earthquakes. San Jose is a city in the San Francisco Bay area, in northern California. To Hiddink, it was a real paradise. At the airport he got picked up by a large limousine. 'If that happened in the Netherlands, people would consider you a pimp,' he commented. American players are given good salaries and houses with private swimming pools. Hiddink was provided with an apartment in Palo Alto, near Stanford University. He enjoyed taking strolls to explore the new northern California territory with its palm, madrona and eucalyptus trees, and the suburban areas with white stucco Spanish-style houses topped off with orange tile roofs. They started training early, from 9 until 10.30 am, to avoid the afternoon heat. Then the rest of the day would be free. 'In the afternoon we would go to the Fisherman's Wharf, in San Francisco. There were a lot of street actors – theatre on the street. I loved to watch the people passing by.' This was in the aftermath of the flower power movement of the 1960s, when San Francisco was a major centre of hippy culture. He also liked visiting restaurants in the arty town of Sausalito, on the northern end of the Golden Gate Bridge.

These were good times for American football. Many great European players, already over their peak and no longer competitive in the old world but still good enough for a mean game, played in the United States. People such as the German Franz Beckenbauer, Dutchmen Johan Cruijff and Willem van Hanegem, and Englishman George Best were able to extend their career there. Hiddink did have to get used to some unique aspects of the American training. 'At the beginning of practice, we would stretch for 15 minutes. That was a little strange to me then, because at that time we didn't do that in the Netherlands.' With two to three games a week, playing in America was hard work. In addition, the Americans took their football very seriously.

Sometimes the introduction of European players would lead to conflicts. Hiddink's first match was against the Fort Lauderdale Strikers, a team from Florida. They had a Dutch goalkeeper, the very accomplished Jan van Beveren. That caused some problems because the Dutchman replaced a very popular American goalie. All over the stadium people held up signs in support of his American competitor. 'But,' said Hiddink, 'after the game everybody realised why van Beveren was in the goal. He was just a perfect keeper.'

Football in the United States was clearly not at the European level, but Hiddink used his time wisely. He had enough peripheral vision to learn from the larger sports world surrounding him; the midfielder could get a good general view of the situation. He watched basketball and baseball games and drew his conclusions. American sports culture was different from that of the Netherlands. 'As far as sports are concerned, America is a fantastic county. People there are genuinely enthusiastic. In the Netherlands people take their seat in the stadium thinking: "Well, come on, you'd better show me your stuff".' Hiddink considered sports in the United States to be altogether different from what he was used to. People were more generous towards and less critical of their sports heroes. The salaries of star players were publicly announced without embarrassment. In turn, players were more relaxed before and during games, which improved their performance.

Hiddink did not display the cultural superiority complex and accompanying condescension so commonly demonstrated by Europeans in reference to the United States. On the contrary, he loved the country and warmly embraced its ways. 'It was a wonderful time. America is a great nation. I thoroughly enjoyed it. It is a completely different world – a country of great freedom.' He travelled all over: Tampa Bay, Atlanta and Los Angeles, from Boston to Vancouver, from San Diego to Miami. In San Jose they had fourteen different nationalities on the team. A land of extremes. 'America. Land of plenty. It seems the cherries are four times the size they are in the Netherlands.'

Hiddink said that he wouldn't have missed it for the

world. His wife and children also came with him to America. They reluctantly returned to the small and rainy Netherlands and would have preferred to go back straight away. Or they hoped that he would sign a foreign contract elsewhere. He believes that such adventures were the fringe benefits of the job. Of course there were disadvantages as well. The work and travel involved pressures that people who work under more conventional circumstances don't experience. He always attempted to avoid unloading work pressures at home. His children, then still young, were quite vocal and expressive. They simply would not have accepted it if Hiddink had handled them in an unreasonable manner.

Once, after the volcano Mount St Helen's in Oregon erupted, the airports of the western United States were covered with ash and flying above the West Coast was prohibited. The only option for the players of San Jose to get back home was to take the Greyhound bus.

> *One of the American players had given me a tape of Bob Seger and the Silver Bullet Band. While 'Against the Wind' sounded through my headphones, I looked through the window of the bus at a world that seemed more beautiful and impressive than ever. I feel that especially during that time I became the person that I am now. I, who was never really touched by the hippy scene of Amsterdam in the 70s, suddenly loved to drive aimlessly down Highway 101.*

In America I became a kind of world citizen. For the first time in my life I saw what it meant to think big. I understood how you could be open to many influences without losing touch with your own roots. How you could see things in perspective, without sacrificing your ambitions.

STUDENT AND TEACHER

Soon after Hiddink helped to engineer De Graafschap's promotion to the Dutch top league, the club was degraded again to the second level. He then transferred to NEC-Nijmegen and worked with that club, off and on, from 1977 to 1981. He started as defender and next moved to his favourite midfield position. It was a time of ups and downs for NEC, which frequently tottered on the bottom rung of the Dutch *eredivisie*, the 'honour league'. Hiddink had his own perception of what the problem was: 'NEC felt chased. When our opponents were ahead, the team went crazy and bolted.' He considered this the result of lack of experience and self-confidence. 'After a defeat Dutchmen lose their cool and start to strain themselves. But everyone in a team has to become conscious of his own qualities. NEC was sometimes too kind. We lacked sharpness and aggressiveness. The boldness of our play had disappeared a bit.'

Leen Looyen, who now is technical director of NEC, was assistant coach when Hiddink played for the club.

> *Guus is well educated but also by nature an intelligent human being. As a football player he was tactically the best we had. He was our number ten, the playmaker of the team. He was the extension of the coach on the field. He could analyse a game well. Even though he was not fast or agile, he more than made up for these shortcomings through his other qualities. Sometimes he was troubled that the other players could not grasp why certain tactics had to be applied. That bothered him. But, of course, it is still important to know your place in a group. And he did. He maintained a good connection with his fellow players. They spent time with each other after games as well.*

NEC players have their own Hiddink stories. It was no secret that Hiddink did not like to run much. One of his former colleagues, Sije Visser, commented on that particular feature:

Guus lazy? He is smart and uses free market economic principles: achieving the greatest result with minimum investment! . . . He used to walk around in some white football shoes that he had brought back with him from America. Nobody had ever seen those in Nijmegen, and boy, did he get a lot of comments on them! He couldn't care less, just kept wearing them.

Another, Frans Janssen, has his own memories of the Hiddink era:

I started smoking at NEC, in the days of Guus Hiddink and Harry Schellekens. On the sly, of course. We hid in those wooden barracks next to the amateur fields and smoked in the dressing rooms. Just imagine: grown-up guys! And then Leen Looyen came by . . . Or we would light up in the toilet, before the warm-up, and puff away for five minutes. The coaches obviously knew, but they tolerated it.

Former assistant coach Looyen also remembers some of Hiddink's antics.

We had a good goalkeeper in those days. But if that guy didn't have anything to do for a while he would lose concentration and fall half asleep. Once, when we played a friendly match against a weak opponent, we were ahead 4 or 5–0. Everyone looked forward, but Guus suddenly turned around and shot the ball back on that keeper like a bullet. He scared that guy stiff.

Guus is a person who, by nature, does not assert himself, but who is modest. He has a clear mind and vision. He is not a shouter, not someone who is full of himself, who likes to see himself in the newspaper, who craves publicity. He likes company, is a social person, but dislikes people who shoot off their mouth. He is no beer drinker but enjoys a couple of glasses of wine. But to tell the truth, beyond his evident modesty, he also is ambitious and tenacious. When he has decided something, you would have to provide him with some pretty powerful arguments to change his mind. As we say in Dutch: 'Once he has something in his head, he doesn't have it in his bottom . . .' I think I would call him 'stubborn in a positive way'. But that's better, of course, than being a pushover. I suppose that at that time he already had established certain goals for himself, with the objective of eventually becoming a coach. He was quietly gathering information. I believe that his trips to America were a part of this scenario.

Looyen's claim seems credible. Hiddink's eventual departure from NEC was precipitated by his employer's unwillingness to promise him a future role in the technical management of the club. He considered extending his contract for a year, but instead chose to return to his old home club De Graafschap because there he would get the opportunity to ease himself into the coaching enterprise.

And according to his own confession, that was where he felt his future lay. A man with a vision and a mission: he wanted to make a contribution to creating a culture of attractive and creative football. He considered Dutch football lacking in 'technique and daring'. In his view, the Dutch game got bogged down in the execution of routine patterns, with spontaneity an early victim, even at youth training camps. 'Let those monkeys just fool around with the ball. The quality will naturally surface, sooner or later.' Apparently, Hiddink is convinced that the ability to play either comes naturally or does not come at all. He also believes that he himself is living proof: 'Remember that I was born with football shoes on and would prefer to die in the penalty area.'

According to Looyen:

> *Football intelligence and regular intelligence have little in common with each other. Guus possesses both. Under those circumstances you can succeed in the coaching business. Also, a coach experiences pressure from many quarters: supporters, sponsors, the club board,*

colleagues, the media, etcetera. To be able to handle that stress and still be successful, you need to have a stable personality. Often, this is even more important than possessing all kinds of tactical skill. Clearly, Guus is a steady person. In addition, he is a good communicator and capable of adapting himself to a variety of norms and values. Contributing experience, but doing so in the context of the country – that's what we saw him doing in Korea. People like to work for you if you are a pleasant person. And he really is pleasant socially. These are all things that have made him into a highly successful coach. I know his father and I recognise Hiddink senior in his son: a modest, intelligent teacher.

For most of the time while he was active as a semi-professional player, Hiddink was also a teacher of physical education at the Princess Beatrix School in Doetinchem. Occasionally, these double occupations led to conflicts with his various club employers, but he refused to compromise his commitment to his students. He was so unrelenting that he preferred to adjust his football regimen to his teaching engagements, as he explained: 'I used to adapt part of my class schedule to football. At some point, I no longer did that. NEC just had to adapt itself to me.' Such an independent streak was always part and parcel of the Hiddink make-up.

Even then Hiddink could wax lyrical over the good old days, that is, the early 1970s, when talented football players could let others do the dirty work of defence while they free-styled all over the field. Football-wise, he is a typical product of those days.

From 1973 to 1984, he taught what in Dutch are called *moeilijk opvoedbare kinderen*, literally, 'children that are hard to raise'. They are educationally disadvantaged children, often children coming from troubled homes or youngsters who have emotional problems and have difficulty adapting themselves to the learning environment of a normal school. It is extremely challenging to get such children to perform well. However, Hiddink was an effective and even successful teacher at this school for many years. 'Those kids had an enormous amount of energy. Often they would ask me, "Master, let's kick a ball around a bit first."'

He taught daily from 7.30 am until 2 pm. Classes were small, with about fifteen students each. Other than football, he taught the children baseball, basketball, handball and did weight training with them. He spent time after class and visited homes to meet parents. His heart went out to these children who grew up on the wrong side of the social tracks. He tried to stimulate them and give them hope, but it was not easy to deal with the often very unpredictable behaviour. On more than one occasion he had to deal with a knife-wielding student in a fit of rage. Once, a student threatened to puncture all of Hiddink's tyres with his weapon.

Hiddink encouraged him to do so, glad that the boy could be distracted by an inanimate victim and hoping that the walk through the parking lot would sufficiently cool him off to stop him from being a threat to himself and others. He also admitted that he quietly wished that his tyres would stay undamaged. Minutes later the boy returned with a tear-streaked face, asking his teacher for forgiveness. Hiddink embraced and comforted him.

Kleinnibbelink, himself a graduate from CIOS, says about this time, 'If you are able to motivate such children and can get them to work, then you can easily motivate healthy people.' In other words, this experience considerably deepened Hiddink's understanding of human nature.

> *He is very sharp psychologically. He is a very pleasant teacher, but he can also be very strict, while keeping his sense of humour. He somehow has been able to find a very good balance between the two.*

Indeed, these experiences proved valuable for Hiddink's future coaching occupation. According to a recent tongue-in-cheek assessment, Hiddink feels he is 'still working with hard-to-raise kids!' – professional football players.

The fear of getting trapped in a routine job made Hiddink ultimately decide in favour of a fully fledged career in football.

> *I did that teaching job with conviction; doing something half-heartedly is impossible for me. But I asked myself during that time: Should I continue with this until I am sixty? The answer was no. Not because I did not find satisfaction in the job, but because your career becomes pretty predictable as a teacher. And I am a bit too much of an adventurer for that, even though I don't appear that way.*

After he left NEC, Hiddink returned to De Graafschap once more, and worked at the club from 1981 to 1984. He played for a season and experienced a coaching internship of sorts for two seasons. He then became assistant trainer with PSV in 1984.

PART III

HIDDINK – THE COACH

PSV

Guus Hiddink's time at PSV-Eindhoven is very important for three reasons. Firstly, he committed himself for the first time, full-time, to the professional football enterprise. He left his teaching job in Doetinchem before moving to the club in the southern Dutch city. Secondly, he put a definite end to his career as a football player and set out permanently on his path as trainer. He worked initially as assistant coach and, from 1986, as head coach. Thirdly, at PSV Hiddink's star truly started to rise. He left the limited realm of Dutch football and arrived at new levels of accomplishment and international fame. Another, fourth point, might be added. The Hiddink PSV years set a kind of precedent for many of the coach's future assignments: he worked himself and his team from an underdog position to one of surprising success and notoriety through a mixture of enthusiasm, professionalism and hard work.

The rise of PSV in the late 1980s is, without a doubt, one of the most striking success stories of Dutch football history. But Hiddink's years at the club were certainly not all wine and roses. On the contrary, he learned much about the complexity and potential pitfalls of pro-football management during this time. He had already experienced how difficult his new work environment could be during his first stint at PSV in the early 1970s. Then, while trying his luck as a player with the club in Eindhoven, he ended up being sidelined for many of the games, as a result of competing player interests and managerial intrigue. He himself said about this time:

> *If I had known then what I know now, I would definitely have managed. But as a young boy you're different. I came from Doetinchem, and there was a difference between the two clubs. Now, I would have said, 'Here I am,' and would have made sure that they couldn't ignore me. I was too timid.*

Another source of friction was that he had a different

concept of what freedoms should be given to a pro-football player.

> *I felt that even a pro-league player should be able to work or study two to three mornings a week. But [at that time at PSV] I could not finish my studies at the Academy of Physical Education, and that was actually most important to me.*

With hindsight one might say that this conflict of interests happened because Hiddink had not yet made a clear, full-time commitment. Viewed positively, it shows that there is room in the Hiddink universe for more than just football.

He returned to PSV, more than a decade later, better prepared to rise to the challenge. He became the assistant to Jan Reker and in that role had to abide pretty much by the decisions of the head coach. Hiddink is by nature modest but not submissive. His power to be humble comes from his not being preoccupied with positions. The team interest is always first in his mind. And he loves what he does. 'Football is so fascinating that you can work at different levels. It is not an inferior thing to work a step lower on the ladder.' The most attractive moment of all was Monday morning.

> *At that time, I could participate in some practice games and get it out of my system. For*

a football player, there is nothing more wonderful than playing, and that stays the same, even when you become a coach. Since I was a boy I loved sport and I have been trained to provide leadership in sports. I love football and I love freedom – the combination of these factors. It is a profession with variety.

[Playing pro-football] is something that I did from age eighteen to thirty-six with incredible joy and ambition. I woke up with it and I went to sleep with it. Sometimes you think, 'Well, at the end of this season it better be over.' But then you get a ten-day break and you want to start all over again . . . Nothing is better than playing yourself. No coaching job compares with that. You get used to it, though. But the best thing would be if you could stay young until you're sixty and then suddenly die by receiving a hard kick from someone in the penalty area.

You have to make simplicity your trademark, focus on the essence and occupy yourself in a very pure manner with the sport. I think it is very important that someone with the required qualities is able to do his work calmly: that he feels at ease even at moments when there is a lot of tension, a lot of pressure. Every professional has to enjoy his work and be an amateur in his heart. The motivation has to come from inside.

Such considerations provided Hiddink with the drive to dedicate himself without calculating the possible consequences of such an investment. He just works hard. 'I can cling to something. When I am focused then I accomplish my goals. But for everything that I have achieved I have had to work very hard.' Eventually, this kind of dedication brought results not only for PSV but also for Hiddink personally. When the old head coach of the club moved on, new options were considered, such as hiring renowned Dutch veteran Rinus Michels for the job. But things were decided in Hiddink's favour, even though he never expressed any objection to continuing to work as the assistant of a new man.

Another point that may have stimulated the PSV management to continue with Hiddink as the new head coach was the professionalism that he brought to the job. Kees Ploegsma was manager of PSV when Hiddink became head coach.

> *It was possible to discuss football calmly with Hiddink. An important point: he could understand the general circumstances of the club that he served – what was possible and what was not. He could consider whether or not something was feasible or not feasible. He was no dictator in the sense of: 'I am head coach here and this and that has to happen.' He is someone who can think of himself as part of a management team. Of course, he*

would try to get the maximum possible for the football team – but would work intelligently and creatively together with me to get the strongest possible eleven together. He would not insist on an issue when he understood it was not within the realm of possibilities.

In the frequently noisy trainers' crowd, Hiddink is somewhat of an anomaly. He doesn't wear a leather jacket or scream at the top of his lungs from the sidelines. He also does not seem to feel the need to advertise at weekly press conferences that he is a genius, as quite a few of his colleagues regularly do.

The evaluation of my contribution I would gladly leave to the judgement of others. I don't like to advance myself by making all kinds of outrageous statements. I don't participate in image-building. At some point, it was in fashion for coaches to announce that they would eat a broomstick if they lost a certain match. I don't participate in such nonsense. It is not in my line to boldly proclaim all kinds of grandiose things. Everyone has his own style, but that one isn't mine. I want people to judge me based on my performance. The business card of a coach lies on the field and that's the way it should be.

Hiddink's enthusiasm and professionalism got him far, but he expected a similar attitude from his team members:

> *My thinking is that I deal with professionals who are paid very well and who ought to possess the real enthusiasm of football-lovers. They should not be motivated by the money, the position or the whip of the coach. If a player's primary concern is the next bonus he receives, things wouldn't work out in the long run. Also, if I have to motivate them daily, it won't work. They should know what is expected of them and consider it obvious that they should perform. On top of that they should be passionate about their work.*

Still, pro-football is a business, and that is something that, especially at a club like PSV, is quite clear. The financial supply-line from Philips, the electronics giant, gives the club an advantage over regional competitors. Besides his genuine zeal for the game, Hiddink is fully aware of corporate realities. This was something that was especially appreciated by company president Cor van der Klugt. Hiddink saw eye-to-eye with him and 'could do business with Cor. We're both street fighters. Under those circumstances you can be to the point and brief.' But this buddy-buddy atmosphere should not disguise that the chief sponsor of the Netherlands' wealthiest club was interested in nothing short of international exposure – the national championship is considered merely a stop along the way.

MENTAL STRENGTH

I watched a part of World Cup 2002 with Kees Ploegsma in *De Verlenging*, 'the Extension', appropriately named for the time period that follows the 90 minutes of regulation game time. At this restaurant-bar in the PSV stadium, supporters can let beer and spirits flow freely to celebrate their team's victory, or drown its defeat. Beer flowed during the game while images of the Korean team doing battle with Italy flashed on a large screen opposite the bar. A small crowd of Koreans mingled with Dutchmen and watched anxiously as the *Azzurris*, 'the sky-blue ones' were ahead by a point.

Ploegsma spoke his mind about Hiddink and their common experiences. 'We worked very well together and truly became close friends. And it has stayed that way during all his worldwide travels.' I asked him how he would best describe Hiddink.

> *Guus is someone who works very skilfully, especially on the psychological plane. He quickly figures out what the established hierarchy of a team is and uses that understanding very effectively. He is able to analyse well during the game and after the game. He is capable of moulding a group of players into a unified team.*

Apparently, Hiddink and Ploegsma could see eye-to-eye on player acquisition. Hiddink's demands did not come into conflict with the financial issues Ploegsma had to consider as manager. The coach summarised:

> *At a certain point we made a clear decision about what we wanted. We made a definite choice for a specific quality, which we felt should become our trademark: mental fitness. I mostly emphasised the mental strength of the team. I expected that, especially under difficult circumstances, some people would rise to the challenge and display a stable and strong character and would truly start to lead.*

This preoccupation with the psychological state of the players is a reflection of Hiddink's own most noteworthy asset. He has certain mental resources that should not be taken lightly. He possesses considerable self-confidence, the roots of which doubtless lie in the earth of his hometown. Hiddink says, 'With what values were we raised? Hard to say . . . Not religious or anything like that, no church values. I think we learned to fend for ourselves, because the family was so large. We had to figure out a lot of things for ourselves.'

He is self-assured without being arrogant or obstinate, two traits that are rather widespread in the world of professional football.

> *I am not afraid to fall flat on my face sometimes. If I had not wanted to take risks, I could have worked as a government official until I turned sixty-five [the age of mandatory retirement for Dutch government employees] instead. I may appear to be a very calm person, but frankly speaking, on the inside there can be quite a bit of commotion. Football can be pretty hectic. If as coach you get in a panic, you'll lose the regard of the team in no time.*

Hiddink regrets that some players lack the required mental resilience. He himself clearly does not. 'No, I've never had an inferiority complex. I always loved challenges.

I thoroughly enjoyed playing football against Willem van Hanegem.'

His experience as a teacher of troubled youths has equipped him for his task as coach.

> *At the school I had to deal with kids from tough social backgrounds, little criminals sometimes. A cold, hard reality where children had to fight almost daily to stay on their feet, but almost always managed to do so. I worked there for ten years with much joy and learned an enormous amount. Under those conditions your capacity to empathise grows daily. It is possible to translate that kind of work into working with full-time [football] professionals. You have to appeal to their sense of responsibility. You have to remind them of the privileged situation in which they live and convince them that this also implies certain duties. In fact, you work, apart from just on ordinary football issues, also on mental conditioning, a continued growth towards maturity.'*

This self-confidence in turn has stimulated Hiddink's natural creativity. He thrives when he is free to test the limits of what's possible with a team. His intention was to have PSV players become less 'task-oriented' so that the individual qualities of each player could develop to their maximum.

You should not get stuck in systems and indicate them with numbers, such as 4-4-2, 4-3-3 or whatever. Systems should be adapted to real possibilities. We tried to present the players with a good [game] concept and encourage their sense of personal responsibility. As a result, they could really make their own contribution. We tried to make everybody as happy as possible so that the spectators would be presented with the best results . . . Players should not just run with their legs, but with their head as well. They should be conscious of the fact that they constantly have to think during a game. Sometimes players act without thinking. But they have to actively consider how they can break their opponent.

I can improve the strategy of the players. They can improve themselves as far as their abilities, physical power and mentality are concerned. But once the game has started, they have to be sufficiently mature to make their own decisions. Of course, the head coach has a certain influence on team play. But once the game starts there are just a lot of spectators and a whole lot of noise. Then they have to make their own decisions. The influence that the head coach can exercise on players during a match is really very limited. That's why I teach players to think for themselves and to subjectively make judgements.

Confidence and freedom inspire courage to act. A team trained by Hiddink should be prepared to take the initiative, rather than wait for the opposing team to do so. 'Through creative and offensive football, I tried to improve the image of PSV. And it worked.' In Hiddink's estimation, the Dutch 'missed the boat' of international football for years. To change, the country had to radically transform the style of its football. That meant, first of all, improvement of technique, a mastery of the basics. As Hiddink put it, 'We can't say that we are the Chinese of Europe and we don't give a hoot about established playing styles of the world.' There was a lot of catching up to do.

In addition, the Dutch approach had to become gutsier. The so-called 'pressing-style' football is no invention of Hiddink's. It was popularised by Ajax, once considered the most accomplished Dutch football club. In a way the Amsterdam club set the tone for Dutch football in general, so that now one can speak of the existence of a certain 'Dutch school of football', in which there is a particular emphasis on the attacking part of the game. Still, this style suits Hiddink well. 'When we organise the group for training, I often deal with the attacking section.' His insistence on bold initiative, on a subjective style, has paid off more than once. It certainly did with PSV, which overcame its initial timidity. 'We developed the capacity to play in our opponent's half. We stopped playing football backwards.'

But the knife cuts both ways:

> *The current trend in football is towards 'total football'. In modern football, or rather advanced football, no distinction is made between defenders and offensive players. The forwards have to actively participate in the defence. In the past, a striker stopped running once he scored a goal because he felt he had done his job. But it is a minus for the entire team when the offensive players only attack.*

Much later, this aggressive style paid off in Korea as well. Ploegsma and I watched as the Korean team attacked the Italian side over and over again. The Italian counter-attacking style is the very opposite of the 'Dutch school', so skilfully appropriated by the Koreans. It cost the Azzurris dearly. They were worn out by attack after attack from their relentless opponents. At the very end of extra time they were overwhelmed, 2–1.

This upset evidently so disturbed the stylish Italians that they ended up trashing their dressing rooms afterwards. Hiddink, a strong proponent of good behaviour on and off the field, could not disguise his pleasure: 'I am very much against violence in football, but listening to the Italians smashing up their dressing rooms, I very much enjoyed that.' And in De Verlenging of PSV, there was euphoria among the small contingent of supporters – Koreans and Dutchmen alike.

Confidence breeds results, and results reinforce confidence. It is a positive spiral that boosts the self-image and the public recognition of a club tremendously. In 1986/87 PSV became the national champions for the first time since 1978. That feat was repeated in 1987/88. Consequently, the odds of the club greatly improved. Suddenly, invitations started coming in from Saudi Arabia, Japan and Curaçao. Fame has its price though, quite literally. When star player Ruud Gullit left for higher grounds, PSV received close to 8 million euros (A$13 million) in transfer money, quite a sum in the Dutch football circles of those days. It became the talk of the town, and afterwards, whenever PSV went scouting for new talent '400 per cent was tagged on to the asking price', as Hiddink figures.

FREEDOM AND TEAMWORK

In our interview, Hiddink's father gave answers that were short and to the point. In one of them, he briefly characterised a major strength of his son: 'Guus' gift is that he can work well with people.' Son Hans agreed: 'He is very responsive. Sometimes he keeps his distance, but once there is a relationship, he is easily accessible.' Hiddink's childhood experiences have probably worked to his advantage here also, because he learned to rub shoulders with people from the very beginning. 'I always got hand-me-downs – shoes, pants, bicycles that had been used by my brothers – but I was never bothered by that. I didn't know any better. We didn't have our own rooms either; I always had to share my room with a brother.' Over the years, Hiddink has proven that he is someone who can listen well, who can intuitively understand people and who can appreciate distinctive human characters.

In professional football, superstars have much more than entertainment value. Hiddink believes there should be a considerable degree of player autonomy. By encouraging creativity, he is very accommodating towards players of unusual talent. Although it is easier to manage a team without such individuals, it is not possible to get exceptional results without them. Only players with strong characters can add a radically different dimension to a team and bring surprising developments to a game. Rather than trying to force his will upon them, a coach must give space to these Paganinis of the field, as a good orchestral director respects the interpretation of the piece by an accomplished soloist. The coach's task is to harmonise the virtuoso with the group. If the other players can recognise and accept that a star can tilt the balance in the team's favour under difficult circumstances, there is no problem with team harmony.

In fact, Hiddink seems to have a personal soft spot for prima donnas and seems to attract them. His insistence on the acquisition of the wilful Brazilian Romario for PSV in the late 1980s is a case in point. Romario's style did not fit the established Dutch concept of appropriate player attitude or required team tactics. Players complained left, right and centre about the Latin American hot-shot. Hiddink largely kept to himself but supported Romario throughout. After the flamboyant forward scored eighteen goals during twelve competition matches, even his most stalwart critics were silenced. When PSV overwhelmed FC Groningen 2–0, team-mate Ronald Koeman observed that the only difference between the two sides was the presence of Romario. 'If he had been on Groningen's side, they would have won 2–0.' Hiddink's personal commitment wins him intense loyalty from players. Once, after his PSV days were over, Romario spotted his old coach and made a stadium full of Spaniards wait by delaying the kick-off, running over to the dugout and kissing him on both cheeks.

Still, one or two star players do not make a team. 'Players have to put their qualities to work for the team, without making themselves subservient.' He tries to create a natural balance between individual initiative and team cooperation. Because it is human to err, Hiddink accepts technical and tactical mistakes. But he does not tolerate mental weaknesses because they threaten the team effort. People should not pass the buck or point fingers but should develop a mature sense of responsibility. Only this can guarantee good team unity. In his view, every player has to be willing to fill in a gap left by another, to make up for someone else's mistake.

One person cannot and should not dominate a team. That applies not only to players but to coaches as well.

> *I don't like trainers who try to supervise every action on the field. I experienced them myself and they drove me crazy. I really don't have the illusion that I can lead a team in the middle of a game, surrounded by 30,000 screaming people. Ultimately, you are dependent on the ability of the players themselves to tactically intervene. As a coach, you have to back up the selected team once you are sitting in the dugout; otherwise you'd better pack up and leave.*

The result of this approach is the creation not of a stifling collective but a group of individuals who feel encouraged to be their own personal best and are capable of improvising as a team, as the circumstances demand.

This trust in other people's abilities and, on a deeper level, respect for their intrinsic human value, is the foundation of Hiddink's team management. It is not limited to the members of the football team itself. 'It's all a matter of respecting the worth of each person. At PSV, we worked with a physical trainer. He was not a football man, but I did respect him, just as I felt that I was respected.' He selected Hans Dorjee, a man five years his senior, as his assistant.

> *I thoroughly discussed game strategies with him; he was more than just the assistant trainer.*

I don't let my right-hand man just carry the equipment. Of course it would have been easy to appoint a young guy. Then I could have been the big boss. But that's not the way I am. I want to have capable people around me, people who complement each other just as the players do on the field. Delegating responsibility is maybe one of my strengths. I also aim at having an open relationship with all staff members. If something is the matter, they should come to me straight away to work things out – not let things smoulder.

Hiddink combines this frankness with a sense of diplomacy. His relationship with another PSV colleague, Hans Kraay, was not altogether smooth. Kraay, a difficult man who exuded confidence during press conferences but was given to constant second-guessing when he was with the players, was criticised after he left the club. Hiddink did not appreciate that and, despite his own problems with the man, gracefully came to his defence.

I find it ridiculous that people make a scapegoat of a trainer. A professional sportsman should have a good measure of self-discipline. And if players have issues, they have to blow the whistle while somebody is still around and not after he leaves. That's cheap.

Former PSV manager Ploegsma has extensive experience with the way Hiddink deals with people.

> *You have to earn his friendship. He is not someone who becomes quick friends and says goodbye again quickly when things go wrong. On the contrary, you have to make an effort and once things are established and you know each other well, it stays that way. In theory I was his boss, but that's not how it worked between us. We had a board to which we jointly had to give an account for either good or bad results. It was a good management team. It was a matter of being in touch with each other constantly, not only when it was necessary. Of being able to philosophise about football for hours, about what we should do differently, thinking about the future, etcetera. He was just a pleasant guy to work with. I noticed that in Korea he gathered a good staff group around him. He has an eye for that: to pick people who can be respected by others but can also be good support to him personally, particularly in organisational matters. He is a perfectionist but hires people who can take substantial responsibility in matters that are important to him.*

Hiddink's awareness of human sensibilities goes beyond the people he has professional ties to.

> *I approach the job differently, both in regard to the football aspects and to what happens around them. How do you treat each other, how do you treat the press, how do you treat children who are waiting to get your signature? Football is more than just a business. There has to be a certain warmth from the team towards the supporters. Those are things that matter to me. You have to think about those things, discuss them with the boys.*

As long as there is no danger of, quite literally, taking your eyes off the ball, a coach and his team should be willing to entertain anyone. 'The door is open wide.'

The Dutch media have regularly commented on his gentlemanly style and noted that he is not a 'dictator', as some other coaches sometimes appear to be. Still, Hiddink warns:

> *I don't think that I am very spontaneous. I am more impatient than I seem. That's what they tell me at home also . . . Don't think that I am an extremely poised and serene person. I do want to work in peace but I will not avoid conflicts. I never avoid them. As a trainer you have to make decisions, often unpopular decisions. But I do not have difficulty with that; I always do things in the best interest of the team. Personal issues do not matter in top football.*

With all this emphasis on teamwork and cooperation, Hiddink still fully understands the implications of his responsibility as head coach.

> *I refuse to make excuses and blame the players.*
> *I always felt responsible for the results of PSV.*
> *It can never be true that I win and they lose.*
> *Either we win or we lose. After a defeat, I feel*
> *lousy. It takes me days to digest that.*
> *I continue to take final responsibility.*

CHAMPIONS LEAGUE

PSV achieved an astonishing series of successes during the three years of Hiddink leadership. Three times the club became national champion, twice it won the KNVB Cup and in 1988 came the crowning achievement: winning the European Cup (now called the UEFA Cup). During the tournament, Hiddink methodically took on the big European teams and overcame their challenges. Real Madrid issued an invitation to PSV to come and take a look at its imposing stadium, including an enormous trophy hall. Wisely, Hiddink refused. 'Our players would have been quite overwhelmed. We would start the match against Real with two strikes against us.'

He also approached the final against the Portuguese club Benfica with the necessary caution, despite the assurance that up to 20,000 PSV fans would be on hand in the stadium in Stuttgart, Germany. 'A dangerous team,' conceded Hiddink. 'Sovereign, compact and giving away few opportunities to opponents.' In particular, he considered the Brazilian contribution an unpredictable dimension. Brazilians don't just play football well; they are 'tough as nails in one-on-one duels'. In Hiddink's opinion, such a killer instinct was largely absent from the Dutch game. After a 0–0 draw, PSV won on penalty kicks.

Although Hiddink maintained his customary outward calm after the European victory, he thoroughly enjoyed the celebrations and everything that came along with them: the publicity, the hordes of journalists, the interest in PSV.

> *It was wonderful. After all, that is what you are really looking for. You want to prove your worth as top sportsmen and finally you get the opportunity. Not only on a national level was there enormous publicity for the players and the club, but also in other parts of the world. Even Brazilian camera crews came over. I made myself available for all of this, and I also gave the players complete freedom to engage themselves with it. This is an essential part of our profession and it does not disturb me in the least.*

After the triumph, Hiddink got in the crosshairs of football realtors all over Europe. His phone ran off the hook. Still, he was in no hurry to leave his old club.

> *Of course, as soon as you achieve your goal, you get hungry and say: 'Then this next thing has to succeed also.' You're not satisfied with what you have accomplished, but keep establishing new objectives. At that time, though, I heard cautioning comments left and right. Something like: 'Don't enjoy yourself too much this year, because next year . . .' Really Dutch, isn't it? When things are going well, you immediately have to be cut down to size.*

Hiddink is the first one to recognise that success, particularly in sports, is fleeting.

> *Professional football is something that is very hard to plan, despite all kinds of ambitious goals. You often have to respond ad hoc. There is no certainty in football. After such a success as PSV's, I could not just lean back and think: 'I'm covered until next season.' He who looks for security should not work in professional football. There have been very few clubs that have been able to maintain themselves at the top for several years in a row: Real Madrid in the 1950s, and later Ajax and Bayern*

> *München, to some degree. At PSV we started working to prepare a team for the 1990s, in the knowledge that you cannot maintain yourself at the top for five or six years consecutively. There will always be some kind of sine curve. You just have to try to limit the pendulum swing as much as possible.*

At the end of the next season Hiddink became sick, for the first time in twelve years, and missed two weeks of training. Other than during vacations, that had never happened to him at PSV. Possibly it was a physical reaction to a season of ups and downs, the very ups and downs he had tried to avoid. Even though the national championship was won for the fourth time, it was an unsatisfying season. 'It was a year of improvisation. That eats away at you. At the end of the season I was completely empty. Then I got a 40-degree fever. It might have been just a flu, but I felt more dead than alive.' After those two weeks, Hiddink felt much better. He had recharged himself, spending time with his son, bicycling. Together they visited spots in the Achterhoek he had never been to before, or had even known existed. 'I like to do that most of all: to retreat in quiet solitude with my wife, my sons and my dog. But at some point, I felt that tingle again and started missing football once more.'

Nevertheless, the downward trend persisted – in 1990 PSV lost in the European quarter-finals against Bayern München. Franz Beckenbauer harshly criticised the PSV game as lacking creativity and imagination. Also, as a result of the defeat, the club lost well over a million euros in revenue. And money talks in professional football. The finger-pointing between management, players and trainers undermined trust and did not help to make Hiddink's position secure. In the sympathetic judgment of Eric Gerets, the Belgian captain of PSV:

> *It is a professional club and they demand results. When those are not delivered, the first one who is attacked is the coach. When things go right the players are praised and when things go bad the coach is criticised.*

At the end of the day, the value of a European coach or player is determined in a lottery that is called the UEFA Cup.

Kees Ploegsma offered a less diplomatic perspective.

> *You know for sure that after a successful period a lesser period follows. Every club in Europe has a golden era and then also a not-so-golden era. With Hiddink we had a time of extraordinary successes and, in those instances, you often wait a little too long to say goodbye. There were frictions. Some older players left, and after a while things just did not click as a whole anymore. Then it really is better to split up.*

Hiddink seemed to have learned this lesson at PSV and applied it later in Korea. He left shortly after he brought the national team to the semifinals during the World Cup.

Hiddink's departure from PSV was not altogether smooth. Some people, including the chairman of the PSV board, were not pleased with his continuing performance and were also disturbed that he responded to some foreign clubs that expressed interest in his services. For his part, he had been irritated by what he regarded as the excessive ambition of Philips, the corporate sponsor of PSV, to ride the wave of PSV's victories to the maximum and push the A-team on a globetrotting mission, advertising the sponsor's name and products. Nevertheless, when he finally did leave, he said he did so without holding any 'grudge'. He added, 'That's a word that does not occur in my dictionary. I am not aiming arrows at any individuals.' Instead he tried to remember all the positive moments of his time at PSV. His stint as coach with the club in Eindhoven certainly launched him into the global circuit of great football coaches.

PART IV

INTERNATIONAL COACHING

TURKEY

Istanbul is carved into two halves by the famous Bosporus, the narrow waterway that connects the Caspian Sea with the Sea of Marmara and the Mediterranean Sea. The European half is populated by some seven million people: a dusty, smoggy, bustling metropolis with streets crammed with pedestrians, buses, taxis and cars that are definitely not up to West European standards. On the Asian side of town things are less hectic and quarters are not as tight because the city has room to grow into the Anatolian peninsula. Always quick off the mark, Hiddink chose the better option and selected this part of the city to make his home.

In 1990, the Dutch coach signed a two-year contract as technical director of *Fenerbahçe Spor Kulübü*, Fenerbahçe Sports Club, the oldest and most popular football club in Turkey. Although he said that financial considerations played only a secondary role in his move from Eindhoven to Istanbul, material concerns were certainly well taken care of before the transfer took place. He was assured a very substantial salary, with taxes paid by his new employer. His residence, in a posh neighbourhood, was a two-floor house with no less than two living-rooms, six bedrooms and two bathrooms. The beach on the Sea of Marmara, less than fifty metres away and a beautiful view of the Bosporus, a swimming pool and tennis court in the yard made the picture complete. Then there were a Mercedes Benz, also courtesy of the club, and the promise of a very generous bonus, also tax-free, if his new team became Turkish champions. (As a comparison of the bonus he received when PSV became European champion, 71 per cent disappeared to the Dutch tax authority.) In addition to all this, his wife could regularly commute between their children in the Netherlands and her husband in Turkey at the expense of the club.

After the conflict with the management of PSV, Hiddink had to look for a new position as coach. There was no shortage of offers. France, Switzerland, Portugal and Turkey all expressed interest. The Italian-language course that the versatile Dutchman had listened to on his daily commute from Eindhoven to his hometown of

Zelham was of little use after all. To his credit, he watched four games of Fenerbahçe before he finally decided in favour of the Turkish offer. He explained that his primary reason for choosing to go to Turkey was that the country has a great football climate. Audiences are wild with enthusiasm, and the admiration of club fans knows no bounds. Even at the opening of the training season there are between ten and fifteen thousand spectators in the stadium. As an older supporter of Fenerbahçe later expressed, 'Mister Iedink [*sic*], I wish you the very best in the game against Atalanta. You should know that I am prepared to die for Fenerbahçe.' But Hiddink soon learned to understand the limitations of such devotion, and would mumble something in response like, 'Yes, but if we lose my life would be in danger.' Whereupon the supporter would smile politely, make a deep bow and, in deference to the coach, walk several steps backwards before turning around and leaving.

The challenges he faced upon arrival were considerable. The president of the club asked the new coach to make the club into a well-organised, West European-style club. That was easier said than done. According to Hiddink, one of the most serious problems in Turkish football was the lack of discipline. Not infrequently, players were individually very gifted and highly skilled. But during games, they would sometimes end up in completely different field positions to the ones assigned to them. Hiddink explained:

> *Every player basically worked for himself. When I started as a coach there, the right defender would suddenly be playing on the left flank. Then there was a midfielder, whose main task was to intercept the ball. He was very good at that, but once he got hold of the ball, he also wanted to make a dash across the field, make a pass and, if at all possible, score as well.*

The only man who really mattered in the view of the Turkish fans was the one who scored. In other words, the player who had the ball kept it. Some things were better organised than he had anticipated, though. He observed, in his light and somewhat irreverent way, 'They were much more westernised than I expected. Fortunately, they didn't observe Ramadan. Otherwise, I would have had to work with a half-starved team. They also didn't stop to pray five times a day.'

In a way, the coaching challenge was the least of Hiddink's problems. Club management proved an even greater obstacle, which, especially in the beginning, distracted him from actual training. To begin with, the club board consisted of twenty-five people, every one of them a millionaire. Hiddink:

> *If you have money in Turkey, then you become a board member of a football club. Because that means that you will get publicity. There is an*

Gerrit and Jo Hiddink with their six sons in the 1960s. Guus is standing in the back row on the left. *(Photo courtesy Hiddink family collection)*

The early soccer days at SC Varsseveld, 1963. Hiddink is standing fourth from right.

At high school. Guus is standing in the back row.
(Photo courtesy Hiddink family collection)

Hiddink the professional player at De Graafschap.

Hiddink as player at PSV-Eindhoven, 1971.
(Photo courtesy Hiddink family collection)

The Hiddink brothers. From left to right: Karel, René and Guus at De Graafschap.

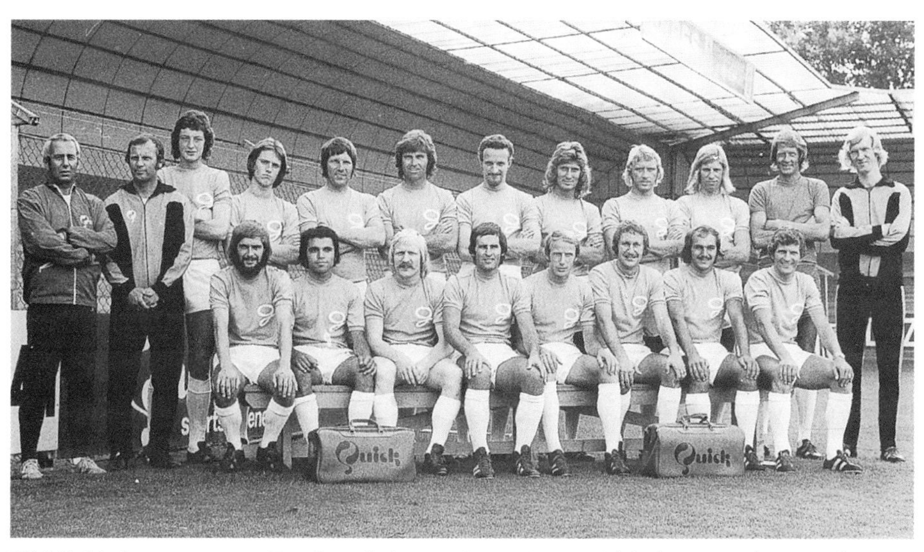

Hiddink's last season at De Graafschap, 1975–1976. Hiddink is standing sixth from left.

On the field at De Graafschap.

Hiddink at De Graafschap.

The midfielder in action at De Graafschap, far right.

Always ready for a joke, Hiddink has assistant coach Frits Kleinnibbelink (left) and coach Ad Zonderland (centre) smiling at De Graafschap in 1972.

Hiddink on the field.

The Dutch media cover World Cup 2002, describing Hiddink as 'an ordinary man with authority'. *(Image courtesy* Elsevier *Magazine)*

OMSLAGARTIKEL

Zuid-Korea is na het bereiken van de kwartfinale van het WK voetbal voor eens en voor altijd getroost in zijn ruige geschiedenis. Dankzij de gewone Guus Hiddink, de coach die als geen ander kan omgaan met vedetten omdat hij zelf geen vedette wil zijn. En dus laaien de vuren van hysterie op, daar in Seoul.

GOD IN KOREA

HOE ACHTERHOEKER GUUS HIDDINK KON UITGROEIEN TOT DE VADER DES VADERLANDS VAN EEN GETERGD LAND

HUGO CAMPS

Luns bij de NAVO, Lubbers bij de Verenigde Naties, Duisenberg bij de Europese Centrale Bank, het stelt allemaal niets meer voor. Een Nederlander heeft deze week niemand minder dan Confucius opzij gezet. In wijsheid en glorie, in aanbidding en nalatenschap.

Guus Hiddink.

Drie weken voor de aftrap van het WK 2002 spraken we elkaar in een hotel in het Duitse Essen. Hij had er zin in, maar hij hield ook rekening met de eerste apocalyps in zijn leven. 'Weet je,' zei hij dromerig, 'nu pas besef ik dat ik niet alleen over voetbal ga, maar over het geluk van een hele natie. Ik ben geen leverancier van een tactisch concept, van aanvallend voetbal of van doortastend positiespel, ik word gezien als bezorger van spiritualiteit.' Hij kon wel lachen om de metafysische uitvergroting.

Vier wedstrijden later is Guus uit de Achterhoek in Zuid-Korea verheven tot vader des vaderlands. Autonome cultuurschepper van een *Korean Dream* die het volk per bliksemschicht loswrikte uit eeuwenlange zelfkwelling en minderwaardigheid. Wat conglomeraten en syndicaten niet lukte, speelde een voetbalcoach uit de Nederlandse polder klaar: Zuid-Korea is voor eens en voor altijd getroost in zijn ruige geschiedenis. Het zou nie-

Guus Hiddink met speler van Zuid-Korea

Korea wil als Hiddink zijn

Met Koreaanse team in Hoenderloo

Oranje-coach bij WK 1998

The media portrayed Hiddink as a 'God in Korea', as seen in *Elsevier* Magazine. *(Image courtesy* Elsevier *Magazine)*

Celebrating fourth place at the 2002 World Cup with the Korean team. Hiddink is throwing his trademark uppercut. *(Photo ©Joongang)*

> *enormous competition among the board members of a club. They all recruit their own players independently of each other. If board member A buys a player, then board member B does also, because he does not want to stay behind. That's the way they gain power and recognition with the supporters. But they never consider whether the team really needs the type of player they're getting. Otherwise, all they do, all day long, is have meetings.* Toplanti *'meeting', was also the first Turkish word I learned. But the gatherings were pretty useless because even before the discussion started they were already at each other's throats. The spectacle can be quite entertaining for outsiders but it does harm the club.*

Some claim that there is a culture of corruption in Turkish football. Older players presumably bribe the Turkish coaches to make sure they keep their place on the team. Would such things be possible under Hiddink? Talat, a Turkish player with a competing club, thought they would not. 'Hiddink and bribes? I don't think so. He is a Dutchman.' Hiddink confirmed:

> *I know that some of my predecessors had been paid by board members who wanted to get their own players on the field. They never tried that with me because they knew that I could*

not be bribed. Apparently, this gained me the respect of the board.

The medical staff was another story. In Turkey at that time it was not uncommon for a club to employ three doctors, whereas one could have done the job. But there was no physiotherapist. Hiddink worked to get some of the unnecessary medical staff replaced with a skilled physiotherapist and a rehabilitation trainer.

His greatest asset in bringing about changes was the power of rational argument. He carefully explained to the board, 'You see, if you organise things, plan ahead, and manage things carefully then your chances of success increase.' One of his first moves was the appointment of a manager as a mediator between the board and the coaches. He also decided that he would still speak directly only with the board president. A victory for West European rationality. Still, occasionally, a more heavy-handed approach seemed to be required.

Once I kicked one of these so-called club doctors out of my office. I think that man was a professor/doctor or something like that. Just imagine: a little farmer from the Achterhoek arrives and challenges such an authority. That's funny, don't you think?

Although football is commonly not affected much by political realities, Hiddink felt the repercussions of the

Gulf War (1990–1991) in some ways. Two of the players on the team were reservists in the Turkish army and spent their days in the barracks in Istanbul. When the war broke out a television set was put in the dressing rooms. Before and after training everybody was watching the news broadcasts. The war was an ongoing topic of conversation. But Hiddink said that the events did not affect performance on the field. 'Players worked as hard as before. One hundred per cent, I would say.' Some competition games of the lower-echelon clubs in the southeastern part of the country were cancelled, but the schedule of the top clubs remained unchanged. Fenerbahçe played an away game just before the winter break against Gaziantepspor, a club located near the Syrian border and 2000 kilometres closer to the trouble spot. Hiddink's team won convincingly, 5–2, and then went back to the city 'as quickly as possible. It is a completely different world out there. You go play and then get out as fast as you can.'

He confessed to some anxiety when the Iraqis announced with much bravado that they would start assassinating people throughout the world and, indeed, bombs exploded shortly thereafter in Athens and Istanbul. After all, he did belong to the enemy camp, the Netherlands being a part of the European contingent in the war, and he was a high-profile 'enemy' at that – with his face in over-sized pictures in the newspaper pages every day. He explained that he lived near the water and sometimes felt that 'the boat had to be ready. And the car had to have a full tank of gas. Just in case.' He also said that once he had a 'vision' when he walked to his car, parked in the driveway at home, and imagined that when he turned the ignition key, 'Boom! The car would go up in smoke.' Then he caught himself and thought, 'Guus, don't go crazy.'

MEDIA

For those with celebrity status, the media in most countries are a handful. But evidently the Turkish media merit a chapter of their own. Football in Turkey is a very big deal, and Fenerbahçe is in a class by itself when it comes to media attention. During daily trainings some twenty reporters, armed with cameras and notepads, followed every move of Hiddink and his men. The German goalkeeper of the team, Toni Schumacher, explained, 'There are more journalists present at a regular training session there, than back home in Germany during a European Cup match. It drove me crazy!' What made matters worse was that some

60–70 per cent of the reporters were prone to an overactive imagination. Once, when Hiddink accidentally shot a ball into Schumacher's face at a training session, all the papers wrote that the coach had punched the goalie in the face.

Hiddink's Turkish translator, Mustafa Ayhan Demir, a 23-year-old intellectual who spoke perfect Dutch, faithfully translated all the lies and half-truths that appeared about Hiddink in the Turkish papers. 'You would not believe the nonsense they printed there. When I made energetic gestures during a training session, the next day the papers would write, "Hiddink beats up players at training."' Because of its popularity, Fenerbahçe received a standard daily dosage of one page of coverage per newspaper, even if there was no news. What this meant was that the articles were filled mostly with gossip. Hiddink's explanation to the small army of journalists running after him in the stadium – that there was no news that day – did not help. The response: 'Doesn't matter, Mister Iedink, we will invent the news ourselves.'

The media went to great lengths to provide news to their football-obsessed audience. In Hiddink's opinion, most journalists would prefer to speak with him for three hours before and three hours after the training. Although he was willing to take some time for an interview with a quality paper such as *Hürriyet*, he could barely take most of the other dailies seriously. 'They daily produced a full page on Galatasaray, a page on Besiktas [two other well-known Turkish clubs], a page on Fenerbahçe, and half a page on Hiddink. Every day.' If he stumbled, a Turkish photographer would already have the incident on film before Hiddink had had time to check if the fall had caused a bruise.

It was hard to keep secrets from being leaked to the media. Once, when Hiddink intended to meet privately with a potential new player, a journalist appeared out of the blue. Hiddink, as a good sportsman, told him that he had done his investigative job well, gave him a break and allowed him to be present at the meeting under one condition: no photographs.

> *But then, while this player and I were talking, quickly, from under his coat . . . flash! Then I got mad. So I took his camera and pulled the roll of film from it. He got down on his knees begging me for the film, saying 'But my job, my wife, my children . . .' My response: that's none of my business. A promise is a promise.*

Apparently, the man had been forced by his boss to take the picture under threat of losing his job. He did get fired but soon found a new employer.

Initially, Hiddink lived in a hotel in Istanbul until his private residence was ready. One day, he was approached by an attractive young lady, conservatively dressed, who addressed him in fluent German and invited him for an informal interview at her home across the street. Her mother was supposedly a big fan of

Fenerbahçe. When Hiddink went over one evening, in good faith, there was no mother in sight and the girl sat on the couch in a tight miniskirt with heavy make-up on. The interview was a hoax. After quickly finishing his coffee, Hiddink prepared to leave. The girl escorted him to the door and then, out of nowhere, photographers appeared. The mistake he made, according to his own explanation, was to pull his sweater over his head to avoid recognition. The next day the pictures hit the streets: Hiddink running away in unsuccessful disguise with a scantily dressed woman in the background.

Hiddink says:

> *How could I have been so naïve? Supposedly, she was a university student. In reality, she was a belly dancer who got by on two hundred German marks a month. After this, she made five hundred marks a month . . . These kinds of things are normal in Turkey. The girl later admitted in a newspaper that it had been a set-up. She had needed the money. But people in Turkey actually find this stuff great, because if you do such things you show that you are a real man.*

Such incidents weren't isolated events. One of Hiddink's predecessors was lured into a gay bar. Once he was inside, he was surrounded by several men who started kissing him. Of course, there was a photographer on hand. The headlines in the newspaper, the next day: 'Trainer of Fenerbahçe heavily homosexual'.

In Hiddink's opinion, the desperate reporters would make no bones about renting storefront space across from his hotel and photographing him with a telephoto lens. Controlling such a news climate was a challenge. Hiddink had some success by making the club training grounds off-limits to the media, and by reducing the daily news briefs to three weekly press conferences. Such measures were, according to the media pundits, a sign of Hiddink's obstinacy. But they did, along with other reforms that the Dutchman introduced, gain him respect in the long run.

HOCA HIDDINK

The joy and grief of twenty million Turkish people are tied up with the destiny of Fenerbahçe. They cry when their club loses or celebrate deep into the night when it wins. 'Fenerbahçe is more popular than any political party. If the leadership of the club would so desire, it could cause the downfall of the government,' said Suleyman Gultekin, a reporter of *Fotospor*, the only Turkish sports daily. He also believed that Hiddink could successfully have run for president of the country if he had wanted to. On one condition: he would have to win more games, because that is the only thing that counts in Turkey.

According to Hiddink's own assertion, his life in Turkey often seemed similar to that of a character in a soap opera. People's football experience was much more emotional than he was accustomed to in the Netherlands. If he ended a training session with shots on the goal, the ever-present supporters would be cheering loudly for every successful kick. On the other hand, when the team lost its first competition game, Hiddink needed a police escort to make it safely back to his hotel. After a defeat during an away game, an angry supporter threw a rock through the window of the team bus, causing shards of glass to rain on Hiddink. After a win, people carried him from the aeroplane to his car. Hiddink commented in his typical, understated manner:

> *It's all part of it. But as far as I was concerned, that was really not necessary. When that happened I said, 'Just let me walk to my car myself. After all, this game was only part of the first round of the European Cup matches.' They live in extremes there. One minute they feel they are in seventh heaven, and the next minute they are hopelessly depressed.*

One of the board members, wearing a flawlessly tailored suit, would seat himself next to Hiddink, put a brotherly arm around his shoulder and speak his mind to the *hoca*, the 'teacher' or 'master'. 'Please tell me, *hoca*. Will we win the next game two, three or simply five to zero?' In the private opinion of the more sober-minded Dutchman, the team would be lucky to get away with a 0–0 draw. But in order to be able to quickly continue with his job, Hiddink's kind response to the man would be, '*Inshallah*, comrade, Allah willing, but please let me be for a minute, because I am trying to have a conversation with someone else right now.'

Soon after his arrival in Turkey, Hiddink went to war against what he called the 'whisper culture', the gossip of the players, board members and journalists.

> *One after another the gentlemen board members would approach me, saying, 'Hoca, listen to me. You can really trust me, but that guy over there, he is not trustworthy.' At one point I shouted, 'Get lost, all of you. I don't trust anybody here except myself.'*

An immediate challenge was provided by the language, and Hiddink expressed the wish to learn Turkish in two weeks. Unfortunately, he had to rely on his translator longer than that. *Oyna*, *oyna* [play, play], Hiddink would call all the time during training sessions. Sometimes he commended players on a job well done. 'Okay, boys,' would be the comment on the field. But more often he would hurl something at them like, 'Holy shit, you guys don't understand anything about football!' Immediately after such outbursts, the players would humbly bow their heads.

I can't stand that, those humble, submissive tendencies of these guys. I think there is a deep-seated repression because Turkey was a dictatorship for so long. For example, when a player carefully indicated that he didn't agree with my approach, he would immediately be corrected by the group – you should not go against the 'hoca'. My response was that I was happy that somebody finally had the guts to openly oppose me rather than whisper behind my back.

Goalkeeper and fellow European Schumacher described Hiddink as a calm, intelligent man who, in his view, would be able to endure three seasons of Turkish football. 'He is a steady person who does not respond to every whimsical suggestion made to him. He just wanted to change things a little too fast in the beginning.' Hiddink agreed.

Turkish players are by nature lazy. They don't initiate anything. You have to tell them everything. In northern Europe you sometimes consciously pick a fight with some players during half-time, to shake things up a little. But in Turkey that usually just creates apathy. Once, when we were behind 1–2, Schumacher and I were cursing each other in German during break time. When they saw that

> *Schumacher yelled back at me, they were completely shocked. But it did work that time: we won 5–2 . . . When I played with them, I wanted them to grab me and kick me like they would do with the players of an opposing team. But the first one who had the guts to do that turned red with shame immediately after.*

Hiddink could have taken it easy if he had wanted to, avoided making life too difficult for himself and still earned a lot of money. But that is not his style. 'I am a fighter, so every day I would wage war anew against all those negative forces.' Erol Togay, the assistant trainer, could have got a good job as a head coach with another club. But he chose to work with Hiddink instead. 'In a few months with him, I learned more than in all the years previously.'

On the streets of Istanbul, 'Hoca Iedink' was greeted at every step with smiles, and people wanted to shake his hand or have their pictures taken with him. As always, he took the extra attention with a grain of salt. But he would smile broadly when, having his shoes polished for another staged photograph, the street was soon crammed with people. Restaurant owners would recognise him immediately and refuse payment of the bill. They would have considered it an insult to take the hoca's money. There was no escape from the overwhelming public attention. His hotel room was really the only place where he could withdraw in relative peace, as long as he unplugged the phone, bolted his door, and hermetically closed the curtains. He was greatly valued, and at one point the club management hinted they would offer him a contract for life. But Hiddink just wanted to finish the remainder of his two-year term and then reconsider, because 'in general, I am not a proponent of long-term obligations'.

Hiddink's arrival at Fenerbahçe ushered in an era of new successes. It seemed that the club, which was ranked ninth in Turkey when he arrived, at one point had a good chance of becoming Turkish national champion. Yet Hiddink's contract was suddenly terminated before the first season was over. Some observers have suggested that this was the direct consequence of an unexpected game loss, late in the season. In reality, however, he never completely felt at home in Turkey and started looking at alternatives in Spain. He was entitled to do so, in keeping with a contractual clause saying he could be released after a season if he paid a fee of 170,000 euros (A$275,000). The problem was that his initiatives did not sit well with the club management. It was considered a lack of devotion on his part, which of course was unacceptable in the passionate Turkish football climate. So while he was still committed to finishing his first year, he was abruptly relieved of his position. 'We still had to play the semifinal for the cup tournament. But the club president let me go. His reasoning: If we lose, I can blame Hiddink; if we win, we did not need Hiddink. Beautiful country, Turkey!' Hiddink was on his way to Spain. *Hoca Hiddink* became *Don Guus*.

VALENCIA

Red, white and yellow are the colours of Valencia's Club de Futbol. Valencia's football club is the happy owner of beautiful training facilities outside the city limits and a stadium in the heart of town. The lawn inside the stadium is flawless: perfectly smooth and vibrantly green. The stands are almost on top of the field, allowing for close interaction between players and supporters – the way Hiddink likes it.

> *Beautiful white lines on the green. They really maintain it well. Compare that to the Netherlands. There the municipality runs a*

> *tractor over the field once a week – and that's it. But people have to enjoy coming to a stadium. You've got to sell things to an audience.*

He became head coach of the club, the successor of the Uruguayan Victor Esparrago, and remained in that position for two and a half years. For his services he received a lot of pesetas – approximately half a million euros annually (A$800,000).

The atmosphere surrounding Valencia was more relaxed than in Istanbul, and Spanish management was well organised. According to Hiddink, while at Fenerbahçe about twenty-five people were 'fretting over the shoelaces of the players', at Valencia he had to deal with a support staff of only three. Still, this wasn't the Netherlands, where things might be considered a little dull in comparison with the 'Mediterranean', as Hiddink usually lumps together the southern football nations. In Spain, too, people are more involved and passionate than in the cool and damp lowlands. Though he was spared trials similar to the Turkish rock-throwing episode, supporters would occasionally get carried away and pelt players of the opposing team with oranges – in plentiful supply in the sunny city. That might have been one negative aspect of having people sit so close to the field, after all.

Following his regular approach, Hiddink first watched four club games before signing up. Once coach, he continued to study the situation at the club and only gradually instituted new policies. 'I did not want to cause any upheavals, as new ministers would sometimes do in Dutch villages: this has to change and that . . . I just wanted to add to things which were already good.' Maybe this caution was, in part, a result of lessons learned in Turkey.

Nevertheless, when he did figure out what the problems were, he uncompromisingly made the adjustments he felt were necessary. He did not waste much time replacing defender Arias, a club fixture who had played nearly 500 matches with Valencia. He put Rommel, an offensive player from Panama who had cost the club nearly two million euros, on the bench because he felt 'he did not fit in with Valencia football'. These tough measures did not win him a lot of friends.

> *First I pulled out a player who had played some 15 years for the club, and then I benched its most expensive player. On top of that, we lost our first two games. That meant panic in the Spanish media. They suggested I wouldn't make it until Christmas. I really stuck my head into a noose. Fortunately enough, it worked, first during trainings and later in the games. You could see those boys grow. You could see them think: 'Hey, so football can be played this way too!'*

Fortunately the *junta directiva*, the club board, kept its cool, quite unlike the Turks, and gave Hiddink some room, at least initially.

He shortened training sessions from two hours to an hour and fifteen minutes and strongly intensified the exercise routines. He did not like the passivity and fearfulness of the players, most of whom stuck to their positions. He rattled the chains of a few who did not try too hard – midfielders who stayed in the comfort zone by making long passes into nowhere and defensive players who sought security by hanging around the goalkeeper. He pushed them and sometimes used strong language in public, in order to 'stimulate a player a bit'. Hiddink said:

> *I broke them down as it were, and then built them up again . . . In Spain there was still an almost military discipline. To put it in black and white, if I had told them to climb a tree twenty times, they would have done so without questioning the usefulness of the exercise. That way of thinking kills initiative. They had to develop the guts to make independent decisions during a game.*

When he lacked the type of player he believed he needed to make a strong and coherent team, he looked for new talent, sometimes globally. 'We looked for a man who could cover the weak left flank. We looked in the

Netherlands, Belgium, Denmark and Italy. Finally we found our man in Brazil.' This was the twenty-two-year-old Leonardo Nascimento de Araujo, known simply as Leonardo, who played in the Brazilian Olympic team and was nominated for the national squad.

Steadily, Hiddink pushed through his reforms. 'I am definitely prepared to adjust myself to the country where I work, but I am not willing to compromise my way of training.' He made no effort to play to the crowd, an enduring feature of the headstrong Dutchman.

> *If a coach is trying to overextend himself, the players notice immediately and burst the bubble. I already knew from my time with PSV that I can work well. Things went well at Valencia, too, but I was not looking for any self-confirmation. It may sound arrogant, but I believed in my own vision even before I went there.*

In Spain, as elsewhere, he displayed a kind of calm self-confidence and a 'be here now' spirit. Hiddink states:

> *Success is addictive, but it is not a bad addiction. Of course, you long for something beautiful. After all, that's what you train for. If I was not ambitious, I would make things too easy for a team. And that is the last thing I want. However, I do not occupy myself with personal career planning. I am no planner. You*

> *can't plan because in this world you don't have control over everything. You very often are dependent on other people.*

Too some degree this self-possession was the fruit of Hiddink's international exposure. In this area in particular he seemed to rely on his American experience. Whereas Europeans are inclined to become frantically preoccupied with preparation for an important match, the Americans tend to approach things with a relaxed optimism. Baseball players, who play up to one hundred and fifty games a season, cannot afford to be neurotically involved in their sport. This works to their advantage – when they are on the pitch they have the calm power to totally commit themselves and do their job effectively.

Despite his dedication to serious preparation, Hiddink often seems at his best when unexpected things happen.

> *For the match against Real Sociedad and the home game against Zaragoza I figured I was on top of things. But both duels were lost. In the days before the encounters with Valladolid and Oviedo just about everything went wrong. Because of injuries I had to improvise until the kick-off. But those games went very well for us.*

Valencia steadily climbed up the ladder of the Spanish league from its initial ninth ranking. Under his leadership the club managed to defeat favourites Real Madrid and Barcelona, which were at that time also trained by Dutch coaches – respectively by Leo Beenhakker and the legendary former Ajax star Johan Cruijff. The defeat of rival Barcelona was cause for particular celebration. Cruijff admitted afterwards that the Valencia win had been justified. Hiddink still saw room for improvement. 'That old fear creeps back in when they're attacked. But it's better than in the past. Then we constantly had six guys playing with their butts against their own penalty area.' The team had practised corner kicks ad infinitum, but the Hiddink emphasis on endless repetition of the basics paid off. All of Valencia's corner kicks were dangerous, and one resulted in a goal. Media and public alike joined in the euphoria. After the press conference occasioned by the win, Hiddink left the stadium at midnight and was greeted with thunderous applause by dozens of diehard fans waiting for him. The restrained Dutchman was moved by the recognition. 'When I am sixty-five I will think back to moments such as those . . .'

Hiddink came to be loved by the public in Valencia by being himself: a sober-minded, honest, hard-working professional. He was respectfully addressed as 'mister'. His popularity even reached beyond the traditional football crowd. He impressed the intelligentsia when he ordered the removal of a banner with a swastika, during a match against Albacete. The prestigious Madrilene daily *El Pais*, 'The Country', devoted a full-page article to the socially engaged football coach, who earlier had put a stop to showing clips of Rambo movies before games. The film clips were intended to incite greater fervour in the audience. Hiddink commented on the removal of the banner:

> *The episode disgusted me. I did not experience [World War II], but members of my family did. The management played it down as a simple expression of the political opinion of an ultra-right youth group. But for a Dutchman a swastika has an entirely different meaning. I could not bear the sight of it. I would have preferred to see a banner reading: 'Hiddink, go home'. I know how shocking this symbol is to many people.*

Paradoxically, his commitment to club development and professionalism caused him difficulties as well. Hiddink is a great believer in the nuturing of a young talent pool and is always seriously interested in the training of youths. Valencia presumably invested in its future through the maintenance of a football school. But in reality there was very little action at the school and Hiddink had the audacity to criticise its management.

> *The boys in the school dormitory would usually sleep in until noon. And training sessions happened only at night. It was a mess*

> *and it really bothered me. In my second season there, I decided to start training those kids myself with some assistants. I would chase them out of their beds at 7.30 am and practised with them before I trained my own section. Apparently, my intervention did not sit well with the conservative segment of the club management.*

Hiddink explained that he simply had the interest of the club at heart. However, his actions were interpreted as a coup d'état, particularly by the club's president Arturo Tuzon. This, in addition to some disappointing results in the Spanish competition, led to his undoing at Valencia. He became the victim of Spanish power politics. His eventual dismissal was carefully prepared.

SPANISH LOVE

The Hotel Paradores is located 20 kilometres south of Valencia. It is more of a resort, a country estate really, than the ubiquitous high-rise of the Spanish Costa Del Sol. The compound is cushioned between orange orchards on one side, and dunes and beach on the other. It offers a beautiful panorama of the Mediterranean Sea, and is equipped with a golf course, a football field and a swimming pool. The only thing that somewhat marred the beauty of the picture, when Hiddink lived there, was the satellite dish he installed so that he could receive the broadcasts of the Dutch channel RTL 4, allowing him to keep in touch with what was happening in international football. He lived in a comfortable suite. The club offered him a bungalow but he preferred to stay where he was. He drove his Alfa Romeo daily from his hotel to the training centre and back.

Hiddink started playing golf, a sport he had spurned until then. Previously he had proclaimed that he wouldn't want to be caught dead 'wearing a pair of those checkered pants'. He had quoted a Dutch comedian as saying that 'Golfing, that's playing with marbles for people with back problems'. Initially, it was a humbling experience. Confident that he, a football coach of world stature, could do anything that involved a ball, no matter its size, he took bold swings at the egg-sized object on the tee but couldn't hit it. He was 'humbled' and decided to take up the challenge. He overcame his shortcomings, and in the end learned to truly enjoy the game.

For all the comfort and ambiance, occasionally things became a little too quiet there. But Hiddink insisted that he was not lonely.

> *My family made the trip frequently, and my wife stayed about ten days of every month in Spain. My family were very understanding of my circumstances. For instance, I was home for Christmas, but felt that I had to be back in Valencia by 30 December, in order to practise for a game against Sevilla. Of course I enjoyed being home in the Netherlands, but I also felt*

> *at home in that cosy hotel. I love to have space around me. I would walk by myself on the beach, read a book somewhere in the dunes and swim in the sea about three times a week, even when the Spaniards thought winter had already set in. They considered me crazy and had already started wearing gloves themselves.*

Life in Spain was good to Hiddink. He lost about five kilograms and found the peace of mind that had eluded him in Turkey. The balmy climate in the city of oranges certainly helped. Even in January the mercury climbed to a comfortable 17 degrees. The first two weeks he was at the stadium all day long, until nine in the evening. By that time he was exhausted. After that he included a siesta in his daily routine, just like the Spaniards. Once he got used to the Spanish daily rhythm, he managed to live a balanced lifestyle.

> *From two to six in the afternoon, life grinds to a halt. Your days were really divided into two halves. In summer, when temperatures go up to 40 degrees, we trained at 8 am and again at 7 pm.*

No Dutch routine with dinners neatly scheduled at six in the evening. Not infrequently, they would eat at midnight. 'Looking back, it was a beautiful dream. You worked without a watch, as it were. To bring some order into that chaos, that was a great experience.' He expressed nostalgia about the days spent in short sleeves and lunches at the harbour with all those typical southern appetisers. He developed a taste for wine. Hurry was almost non-existent in Spain. It is probably no exaggeration to say that in Valencia Hiddink caught the 'Spanish virus'. The easy, free-flowing Mediterranean spirit agreed with him.

Hiddink came prepared, maybe also somewhat inspired, by the Turkish experience.

> *From the moment that it became obvious that I would move to Valencia, I started studying Spanish. During my vacation on Terschelling I continued with my studies. I sat stooped over my books till 4 am. Then, when I finally went to bed, I could see the sun rise. Beautiful, man! I had also ordered translations of all Spanish football terms. As a result, I could communicate a bit in Spanish from the very first training. Originally, I was going to use an interpreter, but we were able to understand each other quite well, even though I expressed myself in a kind of telegram style. From the beginning, I could express what I wanted to, so I sent the interpreter home. My contacts with the Spanish media were pretty good, because I managed the language well. That was really appreciated.*

Within two months Hiddink could have a more or less fluent conversation. Everyone was duly impressed.

Despite Hiddink's positive spin, in Spain, as in Turkey before, the media often provided a shroud of innuendo and sensation around his activities. A smoker for years, Hiddink rolled his own cigarettes, from so-called 'shag', a coarse, shredded type of tobacco, usually packaged in blue packages that go together with blue jeans so well. It is a bad habit and a lifestyle statement, quite literally rolled into one. It is common in the Netherlands but not in Spain. Soon after his arrival, the papers announced, 'Coach smokes *porros* [hashish]'. But Hiddink got wise. At an outdoor photo shoot he willingly allowed himself to be shoved into position. This mise-en-scène came to an abrupt end when one smart guy put him in front of a church and a pretty girl appeared next to him from out of nowhere. Slight paranoia got the better of him:

> *I know that trick from the airports and train stations in Turkey. There you also have those kinds of chicas [girls] who suddenly start walking beside you. Next day the picture is in the papers with a juicy story underneath.*

There is nothing as fickle as the media, though. The same journalists who had predicted that he would not last into the new year were heaping praise on him after Valencia's ascent started.

The collusion between sensationalist media and self-serving board members made a toxic mixture. In effect, the Spanish press corps was the conscience of the Valencia governing board. The club press chief, Vincente Balanza, had to deal with the representatives of no less than thirty-seven different newspapers and broadcast media. Daily about a dozen journalists were loitering at the stadium gates ready to pounce upon the latest morsels flying off the rumour mill. According to Hiddink:

> *The board members openly admitted that they were very sensitive to media coverage. The president of the club was glued to the radio in his office so that he could instantly respond to news about the club. They considered this a type of marketing. It would have been better if they had kept their own counsel and stuck to their guns.*

Hiddink said that he learned to ignore the madness at the fringes.

> *But it was important to the club. The board members essentially had the best of intentions. Most of them were successful businessmen, but they spent most of their time at the club. This continuous presence did not make my work any easier. Most of the decisions these people*

> *made were based on emotions. It appeared as if everybody there was always very busy, but they rarely worked efficiently. The club offices were bulging with books and magazines, with the result that people could hardly move in those places. But I wasn't about to change that – I was no missionary from the Netherlands who was going to tell them how to run their affairs.*

Just like Cruijff at Barcelona, Hiddink had to wage war with the management and the established powers throughout his tenure. What made matters worse was that, as in Turkey, there was an intimate relationship between special interests at the club and particular media organisations. In the beginning, one of his assistants functioned as an informer for the club's president. 'Whenever something happened during training, the president would find out about it in three minutes.' This undermined building relationships of trust within the team. Hiddink soon dismissed the assistant, which meant that the president lost his source of information. After his first year, he submitted a report to the management with numerous proposals for change. When he returned home after the board meeting, much to his astonishment, he heard his entire report on radio. 'Sometimes it was as if there were microphones attached to the meeting table.'

There were definitely forces that desired the downfall

of the Dutch coach. When, after a series of stellar performances in the Spanish competition, the winds of fortune changed, his opponents used the opportunity to get rid of Hiddink. During the UEFA Cup things did not go quite as well as during the national competition. In particular, the 7–0 loss against the German club Karlsruhe caused a disturbance. The decision for Hiddink to leave was made in his absence at the *corrida*, a nickname for club board meetings literally meaning 'bullfight', and leaked to the press before he was even notified. When he returned, still unsuspecting, to his suite after a game of golf, a group of journalists had gathered at his doorstep. His fate was sealed.

After his dismissal, Hiddink stayed in Valencia for three more weeks to settle the terms of the unfinished third year of his contract and to bid farewell to friends.

> *I don't want to justify myself, but according to the survey of an independent agency, eighty per cent of the people questioned were in support of me. I was constantly confronted with groups of crying people and literally received hundreds of invitations to come and say goodbye. The farewell with the players was emotional as well. I had invited the whole group but expected that the reserves would not come. But they all came, all twenty-two of them. They were crying too.*

When he got to his car to head back to the Netherlands, 'the chambermaids had prepared lunch packages for me and all kinds of presents. When I finally drove away, they were all weeping.' He drove the 1,700 kilometres back in one run, listening to music along the way: until Perpignan (a city in southern France), the Gipsy Kings and Gloria Estefan, after Perpignan, Dire Straits and Pink Floyd.

Paco Real, the former coordinator of the football school, had helped to write a negative report about Hiddink's performance. He became Valencia's new coach. But Valencia supporters chanted Hiddink's name during the next game against Barcelona, which the team lost 4–0. The club slid down from a top position in the Spanish league and the president got into trouble. He was replaced by another man, Francisco Roig. The new president soon contacted Hiddink in the Netherlands with the request for his return. 'It was a beautiful moment,' said Hiddink. Still, he was not eager to run back.

> *There were still people there who I felt had stabbed me in the back. They would have had to leave before I would have considered returning. I refuse to let myself be used as a puppet, even if I get paid a royal salary. There was an enormous power struggle at Valencia. Fellini could have made a beautiful movie of it.*

He said, however, that he harboured no resentment against those who engineered his dismissal, because he still cherished the beautiful memories of that time.

ROYAL FEDERATION COACH

After his departure from Valencia, Hiddink returned to the club once more, as troubleshooter, during the spring months of 1994. Otherwise, he enjoyed a sabbatical that year. He bought a farm just outside Varsseveld with stables and meadows. He bought sheep to graze the fields – avoiding horses because they require too much care and that would interfere with his plans for leisure travel.

After living under intense pressure for twelve years of coaching, Hiddink embraced the opportunity to step back from the limelight and take some time for himself. 'I enjoy reading, but for many years I did not manage to do a lot of it. I would always be preoccupied with the next game.' After his dismissal from Valencia, he had time, at last, to 'read endlessly, wander through Amsterdam or hang out for a day at a blues festival'. Besides indulging himself in the solid rock music he likes, he spent time enjoying the peace and quiet of his favourite Dutch island. 'A wonderful place, Terschelling – fishing at night and bird-watching during the day. I can really be myself there. On the street it's, "hi Hiddink". And then I just call back, "hi there". And that's it.'

After he left Valencia, there was no shortage of requests for his services. He was approached by Olympiakos, Greece, and Stuttgart, Germany. Clubs in Egypt, Nigeria and Japan all wanted him. The English club Tottenham Hotspur expressed interest. Furthermore, colleague Leo Beenhakker asked him to become his assistant in Saudi Arabia, and his name was mentioned as the possible assistant of Johan Cruijff, who was scheduled to get the Dutch national team ready for the 1994 World Cup in the USA. However, he did not accept any of the offers and instead followed the World Cup as an independent observer. 'As anonymously as possible, because I don't like to be a focus of public attention.' He didn't advertise himself, because 'I find that something inferior'. He said:

> *There are some coaches that call around the European managers' circuit whenever they don't have a club. I refused to do that. I just*

waited to see what would come to me.
I certainly wasn't uninterested in the work but didn't feel the urge to start again the next day.

Hiddink enjoyed his free time. When he was in Amsterdam for an Ajax game, the attendants at the Olympic Stadium immediately recognised him and bowed to the master-teacher of football, off on unpaid leave. Even the supporters of Ajax kindly greeted the former coach of their archrival, PSV. 'Mr Hiddink, how are you?' or 'Hi Guus, everything okay?' Hiddink was amused: 'This is great. A few years ago, they were cussing me out here, calling me "asshole" and "Philips-bastard". The only job he did take on for some time was that of sports commentator at FilmNet. He explained that the experience broadened his perspective of European football. It also put him back in touch with Dutch football, after a four-year absence from the country.

The new opportunity that Hiddink had quietly waited for did present itself and came from the highest quarters of the Dutch football hierarchy, the KNVB, the Royal Dutch Football Federation. In a way, he always dreamed of becoming *bondscoach*, 'federation' coach, and training the Dutch national team. In Dutch football circles, this job is considered the crowning achievement of a coaching career.

I steadily went through the whole trajectory: I worked with youths, became assistant trainer,

> *and then head coach. I worked with the big clubs. Even at an early stage I thought that it would be great to be responsible for the Dutch team one day. Only when you work abroad do you realise how great the impact of Dutch football really is. Even in the slums of Bangkok and Santiago there are posters of players such as Van Basten and Gullit on the walls of the wooden shacks. This constructive appeal of the Dutch team was a personal motivator for me to start working with the KNVB.*

On 1 January 1995, Hiddink became the 35th coach of the Royal Federation. The 'orange team' had reached second place in the World Cup of 1974, under Rinus Michels and again in 1978, with Ernst Happel. Hiddink did not get quite as far in 1998, but was able to reinvigorate the lagging national performance of more recent years. It did not come easily. He essentially developed the modern style of KNVB team management – with a group of back-up specialists to improve team performance. He also challenged the organisation's atmosphere of indirect communication and political intrigue. In his words: 'They bicycled past each other.' Instead, he wanted open dialogue and honest communication. Initially, he spent considerable time working from his home in the Achterhoek, rather than at the Federation headquarters in Zeist, much to the chagrin of KNVB officials. They did not appreciate being snubbed. But Hiddink, always a rebel, achieved much of what he intended to by quietly provoking the leadership.

SPHINX

In Dutch national team history since World War II there has only been two coaches who sat in the dugout during two major tournaments: Guus Hiddink and Dick Advocaat. Hiddink managed the orange team during both the 1996 European Cup and the 1998 World Cup. Of these two, the former was no great success. There were a lot of personality conflicts among team members at the cost of team performance. It was said that even if few football games were won during the tournament, the team definitely became known for their 'world champion bitching'.

Among Europeans the Dutch stand out as the most opinionated. This gives Dutch football its peculiar flavour. Dutchmen seem to feel that they invented the sport. This breeds the overconfidence that the 'lesser' football countries will automatically falter when encountering Dutch superiority. During Euro 96 that was definitely not the case. The Dutch team was troubled from the beginning by nations such as the Czech Republic and Belarus. Individually, Dutch players seemed to be more concerned with their own corporate interests and star status than with team performance. It could be plausibly argued that Hiddink's accommodation of *vedettes*, as the star players are commonly called in the Netherlands, stimulated such player egoism.

When Hiddink came to the KNVB, he felt that the Dutch game was rather bland compared to what he was used to in Spain. Too sweet, low speed, too predictable, too superficial. 'Docile, that's the word, I think. Timid, too calm.' What he was looking for was 'dominance, personality, fire, spirit, temperament and sharpness'. Collectively, he missed what the Spanish call *rabia*, contained fury, in the Dutch team. He wanted 'football players who were not only good technically and tactically, but also personally domineering, almost arrogant – rascals'. He wanted daring people: 'players who do the unexpected, who make you think: "What the heck is going on over there?"' He said:

> *Especially on a mental plane such players contribute something that is hard to define.*

> *As coach you can create conflicts with such characters to stimulate alertness in the rest of the team. The* vedettes *themselves quickly sense what the purpose of such a conflict is. If both they and you can handle it, that's great.*

But he may have got more than he had bargained for. In the end, the Dutch Euro 96 participation was submerged in an atmosphere of arguments and acrimony within the team. The most noteworthy event was Hiddink's clash with Edgar Davids in England. Davids expressed his disapproval of Hiddink's management in the crudest language imaginable. Even that would have been no problem for the coach, had Davids reserved his comments for Hiddink only and not made them in front of the press corps. Hiddink kicked Davids off the team over this unacceptable breach of confidence.

> *As a coach you have to be flexible, but that should not mean that you discard certain principles. Davids undermined team unity by expressing his complaints to the media. Relationships have to stay healthy. The team should know that I am consistent and cannot be manipulated. They found out. That clarity came as the result of a sad decision I had to make in England. A strong team is more than a collection of individual technical and tactical qualities.*

But characteristically, Hiddink later told the Dutch media that 'Davids is a player after my own heart'. He forgave him and selected him again for the World Cup team.

Patrick Kluivert, the flamboyant forward, complained of a lack of contact with Hiddink. He said that in the long periods between training sessions, he heard nothing from the KNVB coach. Hiddink's response:

> *I knew the exact dates when I left messages on his answering machine. Since 1986, I have kept a log of my daily activities. I could tell you exactly what happened on 24 April 1987 during trainings at PSV, whether there were any incidents or something funny happened.*
>
> *I mentioned to Kluivert that this was not the way we should be communicating with each other. He didn't have to call me back. If something was the matter, he could have called me at his own initiative. I am always open.*
>
> *I expect nothing. No gratitude or anything. But don't say later that I did not make any effort to keep in touch . . .*

The episode is telling both of Hiddink's emphasis on communication and his attention to organisational detail. A book detailing his management of the 2002 World Cup featured pictures of the pages of the log he referred to and which he has continued to keep. The pages were filled with Hiddink's neat and tightly written records of appointments and comments – at that time most of them in English, with an occasional Dutch term interspersed. He writes in pencil so that when a change or error occurs, he can use an eraser to make a correction.

Hiddink had to use all his communication skills to deal with complaints from the Surinamese, the black players on the Dutch national team. In order to steer free of conflicts within the ethnically diverse group, Hiddink had to draw on his intercultural experience. In the Surinamese magazine *Obsession*, published in the Netherlands, several of the players, Clarence Seedorf, Patrick Kluivert and Winston Bogarde, suggested that there were tensions between black and white on the orange team.

One of the more minor complaints was that there was not sufficient consideration for the Surinamese food culture. Hiddink says:

> *I am very sensitive to such issues. I'd be the first one to pick up a bowl of rice and the last one to suggest that you can only perform if you eat a beefsteak and salad before a game. I, for one, do love that culture and that food. When people start to create the image that I don't respect their culture, I think, 'Wait a minute, what are they talking about? One more word and they have decided that I am a racist.'*

> *I tried to be completely open to everyone on the team. I watched how the players treated each other, who talked with whom, and how they touched each other. I made sure that there were no more twisted relationships. I became convinced that nobody on the team had any prejudices against the Surinamese. The Surinamese people have experienced oppression and ethnic conflicts. I have thought much about the question of what determines the feelings and the behaviours of the Surinamese. It is very complex and I tried to keep things as simple as possible. It is also nonsense to lump the Surinamese players within the Dutch national team together. They are distinct individuals. Clarence Seedorf is a very different kind of guy from Patrick Kluivert.*

The Dutch media aggravated existing tensions in the team. According to *Voetbal International*, the self-described leader of Dutch football coverage, there were a host of problems on the Dutch team. Not only 'do the black players not like [Hiddink], because he doesn't understand anything of their culture', but also 'the KNVB personnel [are] very cynical about the federation coach . . . Many of the players complain left and right about the tactical insight of the coach'. They said that it was 'ridiculous' that Hiddink allowed one of the players, Dennis Bergkamp, who suffered from a fear of flying, to drive to games elsewhere in Europe, and that 'people find Guus Hiddink lazy and weak'.

In Hiddink's own judgement these difficulties were caused by his own lack of adequate PR management.

> *In Spain it is common for the coach to be attacked, but the battle is waged openly. The Spanish journalists approach you directly with their criticism and say that they don't agree with you. But in the Netherlands everything goes via-via.*

As a result, his relations with the Dutch media remained cool and businesslike. Hiddink was somewhat stiff and did not take any liberties in the presence of Dutch reporters. He carefully weighed his words when he came face-to-face with native journalists. He showed a clear preference for the Spanish language media, and rarely refused a request from a Spanish or South American journalist for an interview. He did not have much confidence in the Dutch media. He felt they were insufficiently open to his ideas.

The experience of 1996 encouraged Hiddink to make some adjustments while preparing for the 1998 World Cup. He realised that the team could only achieve a good result if he emphasised cooperation within the group. All the candidates for team selection received a long letter from him in which he demanded unconditional loyalty and expressed his absolute refusal to accept any kind of in-fighting on the team. He established a covenant with the team members: a code of conduct containing fourteen points. By submitting themselves to it, the players solemnly pledged to deny themselves for the sake of achieving one common goal. It was an insurance against another failure at a major tournament, caused by typical Dutch egocentrism and disunity. Hiddink changed the culture of the national team and improved its image. The resulting Dutch teamwork at World Cup 1998 was an admirable accomplishment.

Hiddink hardly ever conducted long conversations with the players. He was accessible yet always maintained some distance. Players could say anything they wanted to but only at their own initiative. He would never ask them. Coaching staff assistants had the right to speak their minds, but when it came to making decisions Hiddink listened only to himself. In interviews he was the personification of self-assurance. In the months leading up to the World Cup, he clearly wanted to project the image of a man who had no doubts and who had everything under control. By sticking to his guns Hiddink overcame criticism, gossip and rivalry. He had made the same clear commitment to the team that he had required his players to make. He rejected an offer of nearly two million euros from Real Madrid, tempting him away from the orange team. As another sign of his personal commitment, he quit smoking before the tournament.

He refused to belittle any rival, considering that conviction should come from one's own strengths rather than the perceived weaknesses of one's opponents. In answer to a reporter's question concerning the supposed weakness of the Korean participation in the 1998 World Cup he said: 'Weak does not mean that it will be a walk-over. That doesn't exist any more these days. South Korea has a technically capable team with guys who are athletically strong. You can only undermine that with good ball rotation.' The Dutch managed to do just that and whipped the Korean team 5–0, adding another traumatic experience to the long list of World Cup disillusionments for the Asians. Four years later Korea would hire the very man they felt had humiliated their national team and coincidentally prove Hiddink's 1998 words true.

Hiddink is not someone who is easily daunted. When things went bad in the first phase of the KNVB work, 'I didn't lose my self-respect or the sense that I had mastered the profession'. Also, the disappointments did not diminish his boldness: 'If you do not have the courage to make decisions, you cannot maintain yourself at this level for long.' Ad Zonderland, once Hiddink's trainer at De Graafschap, and in the 1990s working at FC Utrecht, gave his own definition of Hiddink's art: 'Guus has charisma. I know him quite well, but it is difficult to fathom him completely. He does not play all his cards. He has a sphinx-like quality.'

TWO WORLDS

Royal Federation coach Guus Hiddink was focused on performance and concerned with achieving results. He was a gentleman in public encounters, to the point and diplomatic in his expressions. Abroad, in his dealings with media and public officials, he was polite and dignified, an ambassador of football, and maybe inadvertently, an ambassador of the Netherlands. In Korea he was no different.

Nevertheless, stories circulating in the Korean media about his wearing nothing but 'Armani suits' are probably baloney. Flashing brand name labels is a Korean, not a Dutch, preoccupation. The Dutch prefer to buy their clothes on sale at a local department store. It also sounds very much out of character for the super-coach. Despite his cosmopolitan image, Hiddink is still Dutch and not the type to spend his energies on superficial image-building. He evidently dresses well, indeed with so much style that he was complimented for his taste in fashion by the master of Korean haute couture, Andre Kim. He has good taste – but that's where it ends.

In the Achterhoek he is a flesh-and-blood person. The contrast couldn't be sharper. In Doetinchem, at his local café, he is one among equals and wears jeans and a leather jacket. People are not impressed by positions or fancy suits. He enjoys being greeted on the streets in Varsseveld. Others might avoid this type of contact, but Hiddink embraces it.

> *A pro-league football player, and a Federation coach even more so, has a relatively lonely job. You have to do a lot of things on your own. I am glad when I can share something other than just football with people. At home, people are generally kind and normal towards me and they don't bother me about football.*

If occasionally someone lacks that kind of sensitivity, he ignores them and soon enough they come to the conclusion that it is better to let the subject rest.

As an internationally renowned coach, Hiddink must observe a strict code of conduct, rules and regulations.

In the presence of UEFA bosses or Dutch Football Federation officials, he produces polished answers like the consummate politician. He can adapt his tone to what the situation calls for. He knows how to behave himself when the Dutch Crown Prince Willem Alexander comes to call and he will welcome him with respect.

> *I can imagine that he would like to experience the atmosphere in the dressing-rooms. Probably because he also likes to be in circumstances were he doesn't have to exactly follow royal protocol, but can just enjoy sitting among the boys. He likes being a part of that loose, informal, emotional atmosphere. But I am not really straining to be accommodating. I am not an entertainer.*

He clearly lives in two separate worlds at once. He does not have a preference for either one. He is at home in both. He tries to stay sober-minded and remain conscious of the relative importance of his official role. But he doesn't like the company of 'cool cats' either. If things get too wild at an after-game party, for example, he cuts out. He tries to keep a certain distance between the official realm and the world of casual encounters. For a long time, while he was coach of PSV-Eindhoven, he preferred maintaining his home in the little town of Zelhem near Doetinchem to moving closer to the Philips city. He liked the commute because the one-hour ride provided him with the opportunity to unwind and put work pressures behind him. 'These trips were a perfect buffer-zone between coaching and home. Besides, I live at the edge of a forest and can just go for a stroll with my dog in nature to relax.'

Usually, he easily moves from one world to the other, but occasionally the transitions are a little too abrupt. Once, the day after he returned from a successful foreign competition, an old colleague from a club he had played for was shouting his congratulations through his front door at 9.30 in the morning. He peeked through the curtains to see who it was, but didn't let him in. 'It wasn't because of the person. Nice guy, really. But I just had to find my peace. I hadn't quite flipped the switch yet.' He lay down behind the kitchen counter, afraid that his uninvited guest would see him through an opening between the curtains. 'Only after I heard the car engine start did I get up!'

NO *BLANDO*

After an absence of more than four years, Hiddink returned to his beloved Spain in the summer of 1998. Just two days after the end of the World Cup, negotiations with Real Madrid were under way. The club, usually regarded as one of the jewels of European football, had its share of troubles at the time Hiddink arrived. It had accrued a debt of well over 150 million euros (more than A$240 million). Also, during six years it had gone through at least an equal number of coaches. So many trainers in such a short time stimulated indifference among the players: 'Another coach, what will he want?' On top of that, life at the prestigious club bred aloofness among its privileged stars. In Hiddink's opinion:

> *The real problem at Real may have been that life got a little comfortable. Players earned a lot of money very quickly. Porsche ownership was very high. When they were 21 years old, the players would financially be settled for life. But players must be hungry – hungry to achieve something.*

Working with people who had 'been there, done that' proved to be a challenge.

He tried to stir things up a little, for instance by fining people who arrived late for practice. But how much does a fine really hurt a millionaire? Also, psychological management of players was a sensitive issue. According to Hiddink:

> *The Spanish player is vainer than the Dutch. If you challenge him in public, his ego is hurt more easily. In the Netherlands, you cuss at each other and then it's past. But in Spain those things tend to stick with people more. Still, they have to know who is boss. I was no friend to the players. I treated them well, was fair and showed them appreciation and some warmth. But there could be no friendship. I didn't miss that either.*

Star status was accorded to Hiddink along with the players. After a day's work, Hiddink would manoeuvre his blue BMW through a crowd of journalists when leaving the stadium. Once outside, supporters would press themselves against the car, papers pushed inside the windows for signatures.

> *Giving interviews was part of my work for Real Madrid. I represented a company that lives off public relations . . . In Valencia I considered every journalist's opinion. It was an impossible existence, constantly fighting against blatant lies. In Madrid I was much more indifferent. That wasn't out of bitterness – I didn't want to become cynical. It had to do with age. For years I worked for teams that were constantly in the limelight. So there were always opinions about me. Initially, those opinions affected me. Later I just followed my own compass.*

The BMW would take him to Alcobendas, a Madrid suburb where he lived. Then a stop at the Ascot Restaurant, where he could dine on tortillas, ham and manchego cheese (sheep's milk cheese made in the Spanish La Mancha region) with coffee, often keeping in the earplug of his cell phone extension cord, to hold the curious at a distance.

There were no glory days for Hiddink at Real. The

club got disappointing results in the Spanish competition, and soon the Dutchman followed the way of his predecessors. He did not finish his two-year contract but was gone after one season. In the opinion of club president Lorenzo Sanz: 'Some more authority in the dressing-rooms wouldn't have been bad.' Apparently, Hiddink's being 'insufficiently aggressive', his emphasis on building team spirit, was interpreted as weakness. After a final 0–1 home loss against Atletico de Bilbao, the stands were filled with white handkerchiefs, a Spanish sign of disapproval, and with calls of *Hiddink fuera*, 'Hiddink must go'. Surinamese Clarence Seedorf, playing with Real at that time, was questioned about Hiddink's sudden departure. Did he even have time to say goodbye to the coach? His response, 'Man, you won't ever see him back here again.'

Next stop on the Spanish trail, travelled by Hiddink on the high-speed AVE train, was the Andalusian capital, Sevilla. As trainer of Real Betis, Hiddink survived an even shorter period than in Madrid – three months to be exact. Out of the thirteen games played under Hiddink's tutelage, Real Betis won only one: an early upset against Barcelona. It was a promising start but it didn't last. After that there were only losses or draws. Again, he was told that he was too soft. Besides, some were of the opinion that his management of the team was adrift because he fielded a different group every game. Hiddink defended himself against the allegation that he was a *blando*, a 'weak trainer'. This was the label that he had received at Real Madrid and it stuck with him through the Sevilla days. The pain of his premature dismissal was softened by 103 million pesetas – at that time the equivalent of about A$1 million. In 1999, Hiddink also briefly performed the role of commentator on the Spanish football league for the commercial Dutch TV channel Canal+.

Hiddink's high-profile career vividly proved the reality that there is no guarantee of success in professional football. Real Betis was the sixth club where he worked as coach. He didn't complete his contract with any of his southern managements; he did so only with PSV and the Dutch national team. Pro-league football clubs and corporations are businesses. That does not mean that the sports management of one and the commercial management of the other have much in common with each other. The 'product' of a football club is a lot more evanescent than that of a car manufacturer. This may come as a disappointment for those who enthusiastically promote 'Hiddink management' as a fail-safe cure for stagnant conglomerates and insurance against market fluctuations. In particular, for the Koreans, who saw in 'CEO Hiddink' the saviour of the national economy and, possibly, politics – 'Hiddink for president'.

PART V

WORLD CUP 2002

GEARING UP FOR WORLD CUP 2002

When Hiddink first encountered the Korean team, in December 2000, he wasn't impressed. Though he recognised that individual players did possess a measure of self-discipline and tended to be less outspoken than their western peers, there was a definite lack of team discipline. They came and went as they pleased during hotel stays at training camps and wore a motley assortment of clothes. A real team spirit and team unity were wanting. Hiddink impressed upon them the importance of maintaining a schedule and urged them to always wear and be proud of their uniform. At a press conference he apologised for having to cut short the questioning: 'I have to pay a fine if I'm late for dinner. I don't have any money to pay fines, so I shouldn't be late!'

Despite the lack of preparation, expectations were enormous. Hiddink shaved off his moustache after winning the Toyota Cup with the Dutch team in 1998, as he promised he would. Soon after his arrival in Seoul, he was asked what he would do if the Korean team made it to the second round (of sixteen teams). His reaction: 'Well, how far do you want me to go? Shall I shave my head?'

Korean society is highly structured, like a traditional family. Positions are clear and fixed. At work, subordinates address their superiors by using their family names in conjunction with their job titles, never just their names. In a family an elder brother is addressed as *hyeong*, meaning 'older brother.' Meanwhile, both in the family and in society at large, juniors are simply called by name. This hierarchy was also maintained in the Korean World Cup team. Team captain Myeong Bo Hong, for example, would be called Myeong Bo-*hyeong*. Hiddink noticed that at mealtimes players sat in distinct age-groups. Senior players were treated deferentially by junior players and generally received preferential treatment, for example, in the way they were put on the placement roster.

I respect Confucianism as culture, but on the football field it has undesirable consequences

> *. . . The age-based hierarchical system of Korean society is also reflected in football. Younger players couldn't express their own views even if they were gifted. Enhancing communication is an indispensable way of improving team performance. The one-way communication of command and obedience had to be transformed into two-way traffic. That is the only way we could become a perfect team and accomplish satisfactory results. That was the reason why I tried to break down the seniority system.*

One of the first things Hiddink did was to abolish this seniority system in favour of a purely performance-based approach. He insisted that all players call each other by name. When they played a practice game during training sessions, he told them to sit together with their teammates during breaks and discuss their personal conditions with one other. At those moments, he considered it appropriate and helpful if the older players gave some guidance to the younger ones. Hiddink again led by example. Young players carry the equipment in Korea. Not so under Hiddink's governance: Everybody helped, including star players. There was no plausible excuse because the illustrious supercoach did so himself. Pictures of Hiddink carrying footballs across the greens and helping to shoulder a goal frame in transit circulated in the Korean media, and people could not believe their eyes. At training camp he was once filmed setting up the Day-Glo-orange cones for fitness training, the lowliest of jobs, commonly delegated to junior ball park personnel.

What was an even greater cause for concern was that the level of player performance was nowhere near where it had to be. Both physical condition and skill left much to be desired. Some time after his arrival, he benchmarked Korean player performance against that of Italy, France and the Netherlands. He then proceeded to announce the results at a press conference. The Korean media were shocked. First of all, they had never seen such a thing done before by any coach. Secondly, they were taken aback by the results. Physical strength and stamina – 50 per cent; technique – 85 per cent; strategy – 60 per cent; speed – 80; confidence – 60; experience with stress management – 30; communication on the ground and sense of responsibility – 20; motivation to accomplish results – 100; a sense of mission toward the country and to football – 99. Judging by the latter two, the will was there. It was up to Hiddink to divine and define the way.

In practice games Hiddink discovered that the Koreans got exhausted by the time they reached the second half. Furthermore, players needed a long recovery period after strenuous exertion. Based on these discomfiting findings, Hiddink introduced a power training program to build up player stamina. This training regimen was not new. Hiddink had used it effectively to build the physical toughness of the Dutch team before World Cup 1998, which was a key ingredient in the Dutchmen making it to the semifinals. Part of the program was doing some form of intensive exercise for ten seconds, taking a twenty or thirty second break, and moving on to the next exercise. 'First it took three minutes for their heartbeat to drop from 180 to 120 after intense exertion, but [after the training program] it took only about one minute,' reported Hiddink.

One common test was used to measure the results. Players had to run back and forth between two markers ten metres apart to show how many revolutions they could make within a given time period. The average at famed European clubs like Real Madrid, Valencia and the Dutch national squad – teams Hiddink had coached before – was about 120. Eventually, he pushed the Korean average past it. Champion of the program was Du Ri Cha, with 151 rounds. Off the field players were introduced to what was to some an unccustomed diet. In good European tradition, they were encouraged to consume very large helpings of pasta to recover from fatigue more quickly during particularly strenuous training rounds.

Hiddink asserted that half of the game is won outside the football stadium. Players should build self-confidence that translates, primarily, into them overcoming the fear of making mistakes. When challenging an imposing opponent or when facing a particularly decisive moment in a match, players should have sufficient mental reserves to come in for the kill. Some players may have to deal with a unique challenge. One such instance is when a son of a famous father has to apply extra effort to come out from under Daddy's shadow. In Dutch football, Cruijff junior was struggling to forget about the imposing stature of his legendary father hovering overhead. The young Cha had to mentally compete with his father, Beom Gun Cha, who had made good in the German competition. Hiddink urged all players to take the initiative to adequately evaluate themselves and make proper mental preparations. Players had to learn how to dominate their environment and shut out their excitement sufficiently to be able to function effectively.

Hiddink challenged team members psychologically where necessary. He effectively deflated a prima donna such as Jeong Hwan Ahn. Though married, Ahn is even now the dream of teenage girls and adult women alike, and is frequently featured surrounded by a half dozen adoring beauties on Seoul subway billboards, advertising facial creams. This Korean David Beckham equivalent pulled up next to the training grounds in his Mercedes 500, wearing designer sunglasses and shaking his shoulder-length, permed mane in an ostentatious display of metrosexual self-awareness. Hiddink didn't flinch, telling him that he need not bother coming to training if he did not change his attitude.

> *I would accept something like that from a player like [the French midfielder Zinedine]*

Zidane, but Jeong Hwan Ahn is a player who has been made by the media. All players and coaches have to form a unit . . . I told Ahn that if he wanted to be a real pro, he ought to pay attention to his skills on the field and not to external factors such as his appearance or his popularity.

The message was clear: get tough and put the team first. If Ahn could not abide by such simple rules, Hiddink would drop him from the team. In reality, the coach may have had no real intention of dismissing the talented player. But the ruse worked. The proud forward was aroused by Hiddink's 'stimulation' and eventually became an indispensable ingredient in the Korean success story.

A lot of the other players needed the opposite treatment. Hiddink challenged his crew:

Let me hear you! Shout it out! Keep thinking and ask yourselves why you are doing this kind of training. Why are the Korean players so timid? Why do you just do what the coach says? During a real match the players and the head coach can't consult with each other. That's why it's necessary that we exchange views during the training.

A team should build up power to deflate the confidence of an opponent. FIFA [Federation Internationale de Football Association] requires that all World Cup opponents go through consecutive one-hour training periods on the day prior to their face-off. In 1998, Hiddink pushed the envelope by intentionally going one hour over time with the Dutch. Matches begin with a mental attack; when a team is pumped up and players experience a good adrenaline rush, the battle is half won.

MY WAY

Hiddink took the Koreans to the Netherlands, to Spain and to the United States to expose them to world football culture and expand their vision and experience. He insisted that the team play training matches against strong European opponents in order to gain experience and strengthen players both physically and psychologically. 'The most important thing is to frequently play against strong opponents. In a game against a strong team our weaknesses show. In the course of repeating this process to make corrections we can be reborn as a strong team.' The result was a 5–0 loss against France followed by a 5–0 defeat in a game against the Czech Republic.

'I am not embarrassed. It was a good experience. The Korean players have to increase their fighting power.' But Korean fans were dismayed and people started calling for Hiddink's head. Hiddink was unfazed. When he was publicly questioned about what he thought of these games, he responded by saying that they were 'good results'. The media concluded from his comments that he liked the scores and he was dubbed '5–0'. Obviously, Hiddink was talking about something else and was impatient with the shortsightedness of his detractors. He expressed some of his irritation.

> *I don't give a hoot about the excitement of the press. I don't even read it. The only things I believe in are the players, the staff, my strategies and my philosophy. I am not interested in the opinions of others.*

Koreans wanted to see wins. But in Hiddink's judgement a coach cannot kill two birds with one stone. It was a matter of short term versus long term; of either winning games or training the team. 'I think that I have to hold on to my strategy in order to eventually win games. That may not look very appealing, but it is important to remember that we first have to take one step backwards to later take two steps forwards. I don't really care what the people think of that.' In Korea there is a proverb to describe such tunnel vision: 'A frog that sits in a well can only see a small piece of the sky.'

As a result of his managerial approach and in the absence of pleasing results, he made enemies and was vilified in the Korean press as someone who did not understand the sensitivities of Korean culture. The antipathy was mutual. Hiddink complained that the Korean media did not have any 'manners'; that they were intrusive and asked inappropriately personal questions, particularly about his relationship with his partner, Elizabeth; and that they only interviewed star players such as Myeong Bo Hong, Jeong Hwan Ahn, and Du Ri Cha, while ignoring others who contributed equally to the team effort.

On occasion, obnoxious Korean paparazzi may have outdone their extravagant Turkish colleagues. A clique of photographers used a Korean anti-terrorism squad helicopter – to this day it remains a mystery how they gained access to such military hardware – and landed on a dirt patch adjacent to a football field on Jeju Island, off the southern coast of the peninsula, to take unauthorised pictures of Hiddink and his men. When Hiddink told them to leave, they did, only to land a second time at a slightly greater distance. Such behaviour may have been part of his decision to limit access to team members one month prior to the World Cup; interviews were only to be granted after prior notification and approval.

At various times, his relationship with the Korean Football Federation was equally strained. In hierarchical Korea, people who occupy certain positions of authority expect their underlings to respond to their wishes, no matter how arbitrary or irrational they may be.

Employees customarily stay beyond formal office hours to demonstrate their devotion to the company cause, even though they may not really have anything left to do. Such customs are diametrically opposed to the Dutch predilection for personal autonomy, pragmatism and efficiency. Hiddink's personal make-up and management style draw heavily upon these Dutch well-springs of individual creativity and enterprise.

When the preparation for the World Cup reached its more advanced stages, Hiddink expressed the wish to go on a two-week working holiday. The Korean Football Federation did not comprehend such frivolousness in a time of great national urgency. Hiddink's reasons were sound: he wanted to visit the Korean youth league training sessions to scout out potential new talent and size up European competitors in the tournament. But the Federation officials were unrelenting. When the conflict reached its climax, Hiddink told his employers that they could either let him have his way or look for a new coach. He got his way.

Hiddink wasn't much impressed with the Korean off-the-pitch entourage either. Korean physiotherapists did not seem to know what they were doing. They would just let players recovering from injury rest, thus doubling the recuperation period. He soon installed his own Dutch physiotherapist. He brought along Pim Verbeek, an authority in his own right, as assistant trainer, Raymond Verheyen as physical trainer, and Jan Rolffs as manager. All three were Dutchmen. In addition, he asked video analyst Afshin Ghotbi to take apart the 'whole-field-view' recorded during training matches by a special camera, thus unearthing tactical and strategic flaws that otherwise would have passed unnoticed. Though this was initially dismissed by the Football Federation as another caprice of a spendthrift, the proof of the pudding eventually won over the sceptics.

Public challenges were compounded by some personal difficulties. Soon after taking charge of the Korean team, Hiddink had to return to the Netherlands for knee surgery. During the first few months of his coaching career in Korea, he had to wear a cast. The food also posed a challenge to the well-travelled Dutchman. He did not like kimchi, the ubiquitous Korean pickle. The pungent smell of the pepper-drenched, garlic-saturated fermented Chinese cabbage or radish was evidently more than he could handle. A wine drinker, he could not adjust himself to the custom of downing liberal quantities of soju, a bitter-flavoured type of liquor no one exactly knows the ingredients of. He kept up his spirits and his sense of humour. When he and his staff were offered the raw, still squirming legs of an octopus at a seafood restaurant, assistant coach Pim Verbeek commented that he would eat it only if the team made it to the semifinals. 'That's your highest goal? I will eat this when we make the finals!' retorted Hiddink.

Hiddink's confidence was not misplaced. Before the actual tournament got well under way, Korea tied football giant England 1–1 in a late training match, although the 'reds' were behind by a point. They were intimidated but overcame and then equalled. Another friendly, against France, was lost 2–3. But *Les Bleus* had to make an extraordinary effort to achieve such a marginal victory. The Koreans were ahead 2–1 at the break. At that point strong teams commonly exchange their whole crew during training matches to give the entire selection a chance to warm up. However, out of aggravation, the French didn't. Afterwards, players such as Zidane and Henri expressed their amazement over the transformation of the team. The next surprise was when Korea squashed Scotland 4–1. In fact, during the 2002 World Cup the Koreans were able to completely turn the tables and outrun, outjump and outdare several of their European rivals and capitalise on their opponents' player fatigue during the second half. Not even Hiddink expected such success. Still, in May 2002, he said: 'The world does not really take us seriously, but we have a surprise in store for the world.'

On 1 January 2001, 500 days before the start of the World Cup, Hiddink was a guest at the Korean KBS-TV program 'Open Concert'. He asked them to play 'My Way', by Frank Sinatra. The song is a Hiddink favourite and reflects his approach. After the tumultuous Cup was over, he issued a Korean-language journal of his 500-day odyssey with the Korean team. The title was, of course, 'My Way'. That's how he did it – the Hiddink way.

THE EUROPEAN RESPONSE

For Dutch football fans, 2002 was a strange year. It was the first time since the 1980s that the national team had failed to qualify for the World Cup. The same Portuguese team that was defeated by Korea during the tournament bested the Dutch team during the qualification matches, much to the frustration of 'orange' fans. As a result, Dutch interest in the World Cup was minimal. Though all Cup matches were broadcast on Dutch television, the number of viewers was low.

All of this changed when the Korean team began making waves. Suddenly, the Dutch realised that they did have their man at the Cup, Guus Hiddink, and national interest for the coach and his team rapidly grew. The Dutch, most of whom know very little about Korea, quickly 'adopted' the Korean side as their own. Media coverage of the World Cup picked up and soon bold headlines and large pictures proclaimed the victories of Hiddink and 'our Koreans' on the front pages of the national daily newspapers. Red became a substitute for orange.

After wryly commenting that FIFA income from the 226 giant outdoor screens in Korea amounted to anywhere between 45 and 90 thousand euros per screen, *Voetbal International* compared the national mood in Korea to a 'joyride on a roller coaster'. The atmosphere at the street gatherings was like a 'Beatles concert squared' that made 'the earth split open'. The country had collectively embarked on a 'social coming out'. And Hiddink was glorified everywhere as a type of 'new Barbie doll of Korea'. Hiddink's words were embraced by the Korean public as 'the Gospel'.

Once Portugal was routed, the Dutch media really started making up for lost time. The front page of the largest national newspaper *De Telegraaf*, showed the Red Devils performing with the famous 60 × 40 metre national flag while the headline next to the large colour photograph announced 'the Hiddink revolution'. The sports supplement spoke of reigning 'Red football fever'.

The more highbrow national daily *De Volkskrant*, featured a front page with a large photograph of an enormous red-clad crowd of supporters in Seoul 'under way to victory' over the Portuguese. It explained that the Koreans had forced the President to bestow a gift, that there would be no military draft for the national team players, and pointed out that the 'hallowed new class of Portuguese players left the World Cup stage crying'. Underneath, there was a picture of Hiddink celebrating the winning shot with Ji Sung Park.

On 18 June, the Rotterdam *Algemeen Dagblad*, dedicated a feature article to 'The devils of Korea' and noted the large number of young women swelling the ranks of the Red Devils.

> *Besides pop music, they have suddenly found a new group from which they can draw their idols. Korean pro-league football players were nobodies for years, but now they have become cult figures.*

Jung Hwan Ahn in particular was worshipped by female Red Devils.

Similarly, 'Hiddink demi-god in South Korea', announced a headline on the front page of the Amsterdam paper *De Telegraaf*. 'Korea lies at the feet of the man who brought the nation to the second round of the World Cup for the first time in history.' In the sports section the Korean team was described as 'beaming with self-confidence', a far cry from the timid players Hiddink had first encountered.

During the Korea–Italy game the Dutch television commentator grew more and more animated: 'You know what is so beautiful [about the supporters]? There are no rows here – everything stays under control . . . The fairytale of the dream team of Korea, the team of Guus Hiddink, just doesn't stop! . . . The stature of Guus Hiddink is growing larger and larger every day!'

By the next day, 19 June, the front page of *De Volkskrant* showed the Korean team running across the field in jubilation after their victory over Italy. The paper likened the Korean team to Muhammad Ali, dancing in the ring, exhausting his opponent and then striking mercilessly.

'Dutch magic in Korea,' trumpted *De Telegraaf* next to a full-page image of a celebrating Hiddink inset into a photograph of a banner in the stands which said 'Hiddink make our dream come true'. Page 17 continued with 'the miracle of the red mosquitos' and described how in the second period of extra time Jung Hwan Anh scored the golden goal.

The front page of the *Algemeen Dagblad* announced 'The fairytale of Hiddink continues', underneath a large photograph of Hiddink hugging Jung Hwan Ahn and Ki Hyeon Seol. 'Yesterday, in Daejon, South Korea defied all football laws by defeating heavily favoured Italy, 2–1, in a miraculous game in the second round.' It praised the team spirit of the Korean football team and said that Hiddink had given the world 'a blueprint for what results can be achieved by sticking to a focused plan'.

The Dutch daily *Trouw*, 'Allegiance', questioned

when Koreans had last felt so proud and asserted that 'Hiddink gives a whole nation self-respect'.

In anticipation of the Korea–Spain match, on 23 June the front page of the prestigious conservative daily *NRC Handelsblad*, 'NRC Business News', claimed:

> *No matter what the result of the game against Spain will be, the victories of South Korea at the World Cup have changed the country. Amazing images of South Korea spread over the world. Hundreds of thousands of young people who come together at city squares to watch football peacefully . . . Is this the country which until recently got into world news only when masses of student protesters and labour-union activists got into battles once again with riot police? Yes, it is the same country. And the irony is that the team plays the quarterfinal exactly there where the heaviest battles for democratisation of the prior military dictatorship took place, in the city of Gwangju.*

Understandably, the Italian press did not share the enthusiasm of the other European media. Widespread indignation was expressed over what was considered biased refereeing. 'Shameful,' shouted the headline of the *Gazietta dello Sport*, the 'Sports Newspaper'. 'Nobody can accept this betrayal', judged the *Corriere dello Sport*, the 'Sports Herald'. 'No other country in the history of the World Cup has suffered so much injustice', insisted the *Corriere della Serra*, the 'Evening Herald'. But all of this was dismissed by other European news outlets as the whining of a bunch of sore losers.

There was also the clear presence of an element of schadenfreude among Italy's European peers. *The Guardian*, for example, felt that 'it was a wonderful thought, that Giovanni Trapattoni's pampered millionaires, having sauntered in with their dark shades, designer stubble and sharp suits, could somehow be overwhelmed amid the incessant racket conjured up by the world's most synchronised supporters'.

Some members of the media, however, found the results hard to believe and suggested that the Korean team had taken drugs that made them indefatigable even during the extra time with Italy.

Hiddink scoffed. 'Taking drugs? That's useless. I never even heard of such a thing. We all worked hard last year, and that is the reason why we got this far . . . If you say something like that, you better have proof.'

'As for the Italian team's complaint over some of the decisions of the referees,' Hiddink simply commented, 'that is none of my business. That is the common excuse of the losers.'

On 22 June, when Korea finally beat Spain, the Spanish were also quick to blame the referees. Hiddink's response was emphatic. 'Referees and players can all make mistakes. But when a team loses, it has to go home. It has to look in the mirror and ask why it failed. Rather

The PSV-Eindhoven coach advertising German cars for a local dealership.
(Photo courtesy PSV-Eindhoven)

GUUS HIDDINK
P.S.V. eindhoven

Hiddink as PSV-Eindhoven coach in the Philips Stadium.
(Photo courtesy PSV-Eindhoven)

Hiddink crooning 'Summertime' with the Hot & Sweet jazz band, 2005. Guus' brother Hans plays guitar, back right. *(Photo courtesy Hiddink family collection)*

Hiddink wins the 1988 Champions League (then called the 'European Cup') with PSV. *(Photo courtesy PSV-Eindhoven)*

Hiddink buys a Harley-Davidson, and the salesman sits in the driver's seat.
(Photo courtesy Hiddink family collection)

The writer and his daughter, Renee, with Guus Hiddink in Seoul.
(Photo courtesy the author's collection)

Advertising in Varsseveld – Hiddink humorously nominated for Korean president.

In Varsseveld, Hiddink's name and face can even sell soil.

Hiddink in the Netherlands with the Korean national team at the Royal Dutch Soccer Federation training camp, in the run-up to World Cup 2002.

The Australian Socceroos line up for a team photo prior to the second leg of the 2006 World Cup qualifying match between Australia and Uruguay in Sydney, 16 November 2005. *(Photo courtesy Robert Cianflone/Getty Images)*

The Australian Socceroos are jubilant after defeating Uruguay in the 2006 World Cup qualifying match in Sydney. *(Photo courtesy Torsten Blackwood/AFT/Getty Images)*

Guus Hiddink poses in front of the Sydney Harbour Bridge after he is officially made the new Socceroos coach in Sydney, 22 July 2005. *(Photo courtesy Mark Nolan/Getty Images)*

than blaming the referees, Spain should wonder why it could not exploit the weaknesses of the Korean team.'

He couldn't hide his delight, however. 'Throughout the years I have trained many teams, but I have never been this happy.'

KOREA IN VARSSEVELD

At every successive game, the size of the crowd of spectators in Hiddink's hometown of Varsseveld was increasing. During the game against Spain it was still possible to squeeze cosily together into the local cafés, in spite of the presence of nearly as many international media people as actual supporters. But by the time of the Korea–Germany game, this had become impossible. On the one hand, the number of Koreans in the town had increased significantly. Samsung Netherlands arrived with four buses and approximately 200 employees to add lustre to the celebrations. The company tried to recreate the atmosphere of South

Korean street-cheering by installing a giant screen on the small church square. On the other hand, many more Dutchmen were present, partly because of the increasing stakes in the game and partly because the Germans are the old 'enemies' of the Dutch.

At least 500 people were squashed in between the church and the cafés. The mood was festive and, Dutch-style, merrily chaotic. Many Dutchmen were dressed in red T-shirts, 'Be the reds', which were given out for free by Samsung at the beginning of the game. Others were dressed in either white or orange (the national colour of the Dutch) T-shirts with the Korean flag and 'World Cup 2002' written on the front and *Dies' mal brächte man nur ein Hollaender* on the back. This German phrase was an optimistic reference to the fact that 'This time it took only one Dutchman', Guus Hiddink, to defeat the eleven of old rival Germany . . . Unfortunately, this premature claim was not substantiated by the game's result. A group of red-clad Koreans with drums and other Korean percussion instruments, sitting underneath the screen, tried to lead the Dutch crowd into a cheer of *Dae-han-min-guk* (the official name of the Republic of Korea), but this was in vain: Dutch individualism and horseplay proved to be more than Korean collectivism and discipline could surmount. Waiters from the cafés were squeezing through the crowd on the square with trays full of glasses of beer. The atmosphere was so warm and embracing that even a German camera crew received forgiveness for its presence from Dutch supporters.

City Hall was decorated with Dutch orange streamers and Dutch and Korean flags. Most stores had signs in their windows with the Korean flag and 'Varsseveld greets South Korea'. The local florist sold small jars with 'native soil of Guus – very fertile' for 1.50 euros. The store apparently found quite a few eager takers in the visiting Koreans. The furniture store on the other end of the square sold a type of sofa it had named 'model Guus'. Groups of Dutch women in native Volendam [a small town near Amsterdam] dress mingled with the crowd giving out pieces of Dutch cheese, advertising the virtues of the brand. A maker of Dutch wooden shoes, *klompen*, had his handiwork on display for those interested. A young Korean man, who purchased a pair and banged them together to beat the rhythm of the cheer, made it to the front page of the *Algemeen Dagblad*. The sports page had some comforting words after the loss to Germany: 'Tired but satisfied.'

The citizens of Varsseveld and the Koreans took an immediate liking to each other. After the game, many had their pictures taken together and there was a long line of both Koreans and Dutchmen at the local ice-cream parlour. The one policeman on duty did not have anything to do: there were no incidents.

HIDDINK BICYCLE TOURS AND A GUUSEUM

After the World Cup dust settled, Varsseveld became a destination of pilgrimage for Koreans. Many of the sober-minded Achterhoekers did not understand much of the Hiddink-mania, but, as enterprising Dutchmen, did not fail to recognise the unique commercial opportunities they presented. The local tourist association immediately started to develop plans for a bicycle route past all famous 'Hiddink sites'. The resulting 'Guus Hiddink bicycle tour' takes you past the house where he was born, where he lived after he was twelve and where his parents still live, the football fields of his first club, the elementary school he attended from 1953 until 1959 (now remodelled as a sports centre and swimming pool), with a scenic conclusion in the Hiddink woods. All of this takes no more than fifteen minutes, at least for those who manage to keep their balance on two wheels. Trilingual plaques were installed at these eminent places.

Varsseveld was daily visited by busloads of the curious and the awestruck. Korean families could be seen sauntering through the fields of SC Varsseveld with children lying on the hallowed grounds which once nurtured Guus Hiddink to greatness. This of course called for advanced marketing ingenuity and a more proactive approach to guiding the uninformed into correct understanding. Thus the *Guuseum* was born.

The original 'window display exhibition' was viewed by visiting Korean President Kim Dae Jung in the summer of 2002. By spring 2003, it had been transformed into a 'full-fledged tourist attraction', as a poster advertising the Guuseum confidently explained. The name was, once again, a brainwave of brother Hans. He personally made the life-size cutout of Guus – in characteristic 'victory punch' pose, fist in the air – that graced the front entrance of this museum, devoted to retelling the life history and glorious World Cup accomplishments of Varsseveld's most illustrious son. Some of the photographs were provided by the Korean embassy in Berlin. A video/film hall could accommodate up to 50 people at a time.

One piece on display at the Guuseum was particularly noteworthy. One of the regional specialties is woodworking. An expert of the trade worked a tree-stump with a lathe, so that when a spotlight was aimed at it, the shadow produced on the wall strikingly resembled a profile-silhouette of Guus' head. Thus the football master unwittingly even infused the arts of bygone days with new life.

Unfortunately, nothing is as fleeting as fame, and in the sports world in particular, memories are short. The number of visitors to 'Hiddinktown' (the new moniker of this small eastern settlement) declined so precipitously that the Guuseum had to close its doors at the end of 2005. The historical and cultural artefacts have since spread throughout the town. In response to the appeals for ever more data and illustrations from this author, Hans Hiddink, Hans Wullink (board member of SC Varsseveld) and Liesbeth Meijer (the author's sister) spent an afternoon scouring the municipality for the remnants, using knives to surgically remove irreplaceable photographs and newspaper articles from display boards in a freezing cold barn, making endless numbers of colour copies of archival materials and drinking generous quantities of coffee and beer in the process. According to the participants it was *heel gezellig*, 'very cosy'!

On the other side of the world, the Koreans created their own Guuseum of sorts: a museum on the subtropical island of Jejudo with a life-size polyester Guus at its entrance.

HOW DUTCH IS HIDDINK?

It took Hiddink one and a half years to reach the semi-finals with Korea during World Cup 2002, whereas it took his French counterpart Trucie four years to reach the second round with Japan. Despite the outlandish conspiracy theories circulating among some frustrated European football fans – such as the 'referees were bribed' – this feat has been recognised as something quite extraordinary in most other parts of the world. There indeed was some justification for the ensuing 'Hiddink fever'. As a natural consequence, people also became quite interested in his country of origin, the Netherlands. Some multinational Dutch companies such as Phillips and ING have benefited from a certain Hiddink ripple effect. The stereotypical picture of Dutchmen in wooden shoes bicycling along the dikes is an enduring one. But whereas the country was hitherto widely known only as a location abundant with windmills and tulips and, maybe, the origin of some quality cheese, it has gained credibility as the home of people with inherent leadership ability. Though there is some danger in trying to identify universal characteristics of any people, still every national psychology has certain features that set it apart from those of others. What then makes the Dutch different and to what extent is Hiddink a representative example of 'Dutchness'?

After World Cup 2002, Koreans took a second look at the world map and located the Netherlands at the north-western corner of Europe, between its better known neighbours, Britain, France and Germany. Besides being surrounded by great powers, the Netherlands, or 'Holland', as the country is tenderly nicknamed by its inhabitants, is also embraced by water on many sides. The country is almost entirely flat, and in many places the land is well below sea level. As a result, the Dutch have frequently had to wage war with enemies of two types – political opponents and the natural elements. This has made them resilient, enterprising and creative. The Netherlands have been invaded on numerous occasions. The Spanish King Phillip II, the French Emperor Napoleon, and Germany under Hitler all marched armies straight across the little country, but all were eventually successfully repelled. In many places the Dutch have expanded their territory by reclaiming land from the sea through the creation of *polders* [low-lying tracts of land that form an artificial hydrological entity]. The Dutch occasionally proclaim, somewhat presumptuously, that 'God created the world, but the Dutch created Holland'. The permanent struggles with human neighbours and nature have made the Dutch tenacious, stubborn, and, in a way, rebellious. The Dutch call it *eigenwijs*, which literally means 'self-wise'. There is a natural inclination among the people to want to defy the odds.

This trait is exquisitely personified in Guus Hiddink. Being very much in the public arena, he is always surrounded by people who are ready to give advice on how to manage things. When he was working abroad, in Turkey, Spain or Korea, people understandably assumed that he would be in need of such counsel because of his unfamiliarity with the local culture and customs. But, being a true Dutchman, he ignored the advice and persistently followed his own way, because he knew that his way was best!

This stubbornness does not mean that Dutchmen are inflexible while pursuing their objectives. On the contrary, just as the water that surrounds them everywhere will quickly fill up any void, the pragmatic Dutch readily adapt to changing circumstances, even if these present them with a completely new challenge. While they have often defied the strong countries surrounding them, they have just as often tried to negotiate settlements, thus avoiding the need for armed conflict and learning in the process. This ability to find a happy medium has often been very useful to the Dutch in international relations. Whereas the Portuguese intransigently tried to impose their Catholicism on their Japanese trading partners and were consequently booted out of the empire, the Dutch managed to secure exclusive trading rights and nurtured a delicate partnership with the Japanese court during the two centuries preceding the Meiji Restoration. The combination of individualism and adaptability makes Dutchmen capable of working effectively in foreign countries and cultures, even alone. They quickly understand enough of their host nation to at least get along well. Hiddink possesses this quality and can easily make his home in a place that was completely foreign to him only a short time before. He has proved his skill in this area during his repeated ventures abroad.

An extension of this ability to absorb the ways of others is the Dutch knack for learning foreign languages. Children in the Netherlands are required to study three foreign languages – English, German and French – for at least part of their high school years. At some point, they may select one or two of these for further study and drop others. This educational tradition was made necessary because of the large language areas that encroach upon a small area of Dutch speakers. And because the British, Germans and French will not (and usually cannot) speak

Dutch, the Dutch will simply speak the other languages instead. At various times, Hiddink's foreign hosts have considered it a mark of Hiddink's intellectual prowess that he speaks four or five languages more or less fluently. Though this is more than the average Dutchman masters, this is a feat not at all uncommon among the more educated Dutch, and few people in the Netherlands would be very impressed with such linguistic versatility.

Still, the feature helps the Dutch to get around, and together with the others mentioned here, makes Dutch football coaches a wanted commodity in the international football circuit. World Cup 2006 will see no less than four Dutchmen in the dugout: Guus Hiddink with Australia, Marco van Basten with the Netherlands, Dick Advocaat with Korea, and Leo Beenhakker with Trinidad and Tobago. This is matched by no other nation – not bad for the little 'polder' on the North Sea.

The geography of the Netherlands has left its mark on Dutch thinking in more than one way. In imitation of the surrounding flat lands, with a total absence of upward lines (the largest 'mountain' in the very south-eastern corner of the country, is almost exactly the same height as Uluru, though significantly less prominent), the Dutch mind has an innate aversion towards hierarchy. Mountainless Holland is completely 'horizontal'. This trait is manifested on all levels of society; even the Dutch royals are no exception. Although the Dutch generally appreciate the Orange Nassau family and were particularly fond of the recently deceased Queen Mother, this respect will never turn into a feeling of profound admiration or devotion. The current Dutch queen is expected to conduct herself in a manner more or less the same as every other Dutch citizen. The royals understand this, and correspondingly behave with modesty and temperance. In a similar way, while Hiddink immediately challenged the established hierarchy of the Korean national team and insisted on exclusive performance-based placement of players, at the same time he never allowed himself to be put on a pedestal (except in statue form!). Television images were broadcast of his refusal to allow a Korean assistant to carry his jacket for him. This is typically Dutch: of course I carry my own coat, just as *everybody else does*. Once back in the Netherlands, he was congratulated on his accomplishment in Korea but was 'just Guus', as before.

There is one more reason for the Dutch tendency towards social democracy and that is the Protestant–Christian root of the country. Before the glory of God 'all men have fallen short'. These collective shortcomings make, firstly, all people equal and, secondly, pedantic folks suspect; people with 'attitudes' are not taken seriously, at best, or ridiculed, at worst. Though most Dutchmen and Dutchwomen are quite secular-minded these days, this original Protestant egalitarianism has left its mark on people's thinking. No one should assume that he or she is any better than anyone else. The Calvinistic brand of Christianity has brought along a host of other 'Dutch' virtues, such as honesty, reliability and a strong work ethic. Several of these qualities are increasingly compromised by the young, urban, internationalised generation, but people in smaller towns and the elder generation are still committed to them. Hiddink, as one of the old school, embodies all of them. He is honest and direct with all his co-workers, and straightforward both with his superiors and his subordinates. He is devoted to his job and committed to the responsible fulfilment of the tasks required of him. Above all, he is a very hard worker.

Dutch people love *gezelligheid*. They proudly assert that it is impossible to translate this word properly and there is some truth in the claim. Its closest English equivalent, 'cosiness', doesn't adequately capture the feeling of being close-in, warm, comfortable, easy, relaxed, kind, and familiar that is implied by the Dutch word. The Dutch reserve this word for describing the happy and casual atmosphere created by, for example, a family gathered for a birthday party, friends crowding a neighbourhood café or women out shopping together on a sunny afternoon. Hiddink is a Dutchman, so naturally, he also loves *gezelligheid*: the warm intimacy of a limited circle of friends and acquaintances in familiar surroundings. One of the first things he does whenever he gets back to 'Holland' (which sounds a lot more *gezellig* than 'the Netherlands') from another foreign expedition is to stop by at his local café in Doetinchem.

Hiddink has seen and been touched by too much of the

world beyond the Netherlands to remain unaffected by the experience. In fact, his urge to look outside the boundaries of the little European country is in itself an admission that 'being Dutch' is just not enough for him. This thirst for broader experience and a larger perspective is something that many other 'internationalised' Dutchmen can understand very well. The Netherlands really is a very nice and pretty country, but it has at least one major shortcoming which is that it is very small. It fits approximately 185 times into Australia. Just as the national geography has impressed itself on the Dutch psychology in other ways, this smallness has affected the mental landscape of a good number of the inhabitants of the Netherlands. There is a certain provincialism to be detected in the Dutch mind-set. The same stubborn belief in the correctness of one's own view of things, described above, often turns into a distinct narrow-mindedness: 'My way is really the only sensible way.' Some more sophisticated and cosmopolitan Dutchmen, including Hiddink, have sought inspiration and mind-expanding experiences beyond the confines of the Dutch borders.

This is part of the reason why Hiddink went to America. America, 'home of the free', has room for innovation and experimentation that the average Dutch national could never even dream of. The sheer space of the country is a breath of fresh air for people accustomed to living packed together with 16 million people on a piece of flatlands much smaller than most US states. The mountains make a person look up to far horizons, unlike in the Netherlands, where the horizon is always a straight line and people's vision is mostly directed to the earth immediately in front of their feet. Hiddink thrived in this natural and social atmosphere of unbridled opportunity for growth and expansion. I am convinced that his original creative genius received an important new impulse in America. There is little doubt that his American days have also prepared him better for working in Australia, not just because of the common language but also because of the free-spirited, enterprising nature of the inhabitants of both countries.

The Dutch are firm believers in *nuchterheid*, the sober-minded rationalism that was so well represented in their greatest thinker, Erasmus. Dutchmen consider it inappropriate to allow oneself to be overwhelmed by one's emotions. The television audience in the Netherlands gets somewhat bewildered by Brazilian exuberance, the free flow of emotion expressed by Cameroonians, and recently, the intense national passion demonstrated by Koreans during the World Cup games. In the case of the latter, words such as 'hysteria' and 'craziness' were repeatedly heard in the Dutch media. It is important to note that they were not heard from Guus Hiddink. He is, like his countrymen, a person in control of his feelings and he does not show them easily. Still, and this may be one of the more interesting contradictions in this man, he is no believer in stifling human emotion. On the contrary, he has always been keenly aware of the importance of sports in general and football in particular as an outlet for pent-up energies and stress. He consciously takes into account and warmly embraces the supporters in and out of the stadium as an essential and integral part of the football enterprise and feels personally drawn to them.

This attraction to warmth and to 'passion' – a word that prominently features in the Hiddink vocabulary; he has frequently criticised Dutch football as being 'passionless' – was what has stimulated Hiddink's enduring love affair with the Latin nations. He found something in the Spanish and South Americans that was sorely lacking in the all-too-sober and rational Dutch: spontaneity, enthusiasm and warm humanity. The nights spent with friends on the terraces of Valencia and Sevilla were unplanned and unrestricted by Dutch considerations of schedules and propriety. They were liberating.

But Hiddink always comes back to the Netherlands and his own niche in the Achterhoek. He brings the freedom he found elsewhere back home with him. He does not 'go Dutch' in his home café. Actually, no one in the Netherlands does. (This is a piece of pervasive disinformation spread by British detractors of the Dutch during the era of colonial competition in the eastern United States. The expression stuck in the American-English vernacular and is more telling of US social customs than it is of Dutch.) On average, the Dutch are not known for their generosity. Some might even call them stingy. But when they are together on an evening out, they pay for each other. Everyone takes turns, nobody keeps count. *Reuze gezellig*, really cosy. This is one part of the the real cooperation and team spirit Guus Hiddink is such a great believer in: you cover each other. You are part of one team. That's how you win.

HOMING PIGEON 2

After the glory days of the World Cup came to a close, hopes were high in Korea that Hiddink, even if he was not going to run for national president, at least would stick around in some capacity to help elevate the lacklustre Korean football competition. But the Dutch 'football god' nevertheless left the peninsula as planned and was, according to his own admission, 'glad to take a tumble from the pedestal' upon his return to the Netherlands. He immediately consented to a new two-year alliance with his old club; an airborne agreement was made with PSV chairman Harry van Raaij during the twenty-minute trip on a Philips jet from

Amsterdam-Schiphol International Airport to the municipal airport of Eindhoven. Two pilots and Kees Ploegsma, now turned Hiddink business consultant, were witnesses. Later Hiddink confessed to being 'happy to be back in the old nest of this ambitious, serious and warm club'. So happy, evidently, that he at long last made the move from his familiar surroundings in the Achterhoek to a new home in Brabant, close to the club.

Still, he had some trouble readjusting himself to the speed of the Netherlands, or lack thereof. An advertisement deal with Philips foundered because, according to the coach, the electronics giant was dragging its feat. The Korean 'palli, palli!' – 'quickly-quickly' – clearly worked better for Hiddink. He closed advertisement contracts with Samsung, ironically one of Philips' main competitors; with Kyobo, Korea's largest life insurance company; and accepted a role as official adviser to the Korean football federation. The three deals paid him approximately 2.8 million euros (A$4.5 million).

There were less serious concerns such as what to do with a boat-length (20 metre) limousine that the Korean company Hyundai insisted on giving to him. He kindly suggested that they instead donate the vehicle to a Korean orphanage, but that was taken as an insult by the well-intentioned giver. When the car was eventually shipped to the Netherlands, Hiddink was afraid that he would be ridiculed by the plainspoken Dutch. Lighthearted suggestions did indeed follow. Why not pass on the car to one particularly swinging member of the royal family or to

Al Qaeda as a new headquarters for the highly mobile chief of the terrorist organisation, Bin Laden?

And there were very serious concerns. Hiddink received several letters with death threats. These contained .22 calibre bullets and were probably sent by some 'borderline insane' (a quote from Hiddink) supporter of a competing Dutch club. The lunatic, who harassed some other notables of the Dutch football world, was eventually apprehended by the police. Apparently Hiddink was so unsettled by the events that he at one point considered retiring from his coaching career and withdrawing to Spain.

Coaches respond differently to team failure. Former PSV coach Dick Advocaat (Hiddink's successor in Korea) would organise training the day after a bad game as punishment. When Hiddink encountered some bumps in the PSV road, he was more lenient. He had games filmed with special cameras – the zoom-in zoom-out images of regular TV channels were useless in his opinion. After a disappointing performance he would allow players a couple of days to come to their senses and then analyse the film together.

The Hiddink recipe worked once more. During the 2002–2003 season, PSV became national champion. Nothing new for the club – it had done so sixteen times before. Still, goalie Ronald Waterreus thought Hiddink helped to lift the atmosphere at the club. 'That season the relationship between technical staff and the players was excellent. The interaction became much more fluid.

That was the accomplishment of Guus Hiddink. You would easily drop in on him for coffee and naturally talk about the game.' At an appreciation ceremony in front of Eindhoven's city hall the public expressed its gratitude: *Guusje bedankt! Guusje bedankt!* 'Thanks, little Guus!' Hiddink took a small bow in response. 'He's still got that from Korea,' observed one of the celebrators.

Not everything was coming up roses, however. PSV lost badly during the 2003/2004 Champions League – 0–4 against Arsenal and 1–3 against Borussia Dortmund. This painfully proved that after half a dozen earlier failed attempts to make it to the second round of the League, the club still had work to do in order to play the big European boys.

RECONSTRUCTION COACH

In European football, with its volatile ethnic mix, the potential for racism lurks just beneath the surface. In 2004, suggestions were made in public that PSV wasn't clean in this respect. Hiddink dismissed the allegations by saying that the team had a 'yellow Korean, black Peruvian and a pale-white, bald Dane'. As if to rub that in, shortly thereafter he was given a Spanish civic award for his peacemaking missions – his intercultural accomplishments in Korea and his insistence that banners with racist slurs be removed in Valencia, years earlier.

In reality, PSV was always an open house for non-natives. In the 1920s Austrians dominated the foreign contingent; the British in the 1950s; and the Scandinavians in the 1970s and 1980s. After the fall of the Berlin Wall, eastern Europeans of all stripes streamed through the gates. The 2004 roster was more colourful than ever. Park and Lee had come from Korea in Hiddink's wake, and the master's weak spot for Brazilian flamboyance was betrayed through the presence of no less than three players from the land of Pele – Leandro, Gomez and Alex. Then there were Farfan from Peru, Beasley from the US, Coe from Australia, Vonlanthen with his half-Colombian heritage and Addo from Ghana.

This imported talent, combined with the solid experience of Dutchmen such as Cocu and van Bommel led to a breakthrough. In November 2004, PSV dispelled the ghosts of the past and, after a draw with Arsenal, made it to the second round of the Champions League for the first time in its history. This was Hiddink's doing. Recognising player quality and building up human and athletic resources are definite Hiddink strengths. PSV was considered the dark horse of the tournament; every other team of the remaining sixteen had a budget far larger than the Dutch club. Through timely scouting and smart player acquisition, and without spending a fortune, Hiddink carefully prepared the PSV incursion. After the team skilfully and decisively eliminated Monaco and Lyon, the challenge was frustrated in the semifinal against AC Milan.

Interest in the Dutch–Italian match was enormous. Prior to the game, the grounds at the PSV training centre

De Herdgang were packed with supporters – there was no space in the parking lot for days. The actual game at the Philips Stadium was broadcast live to some 120 nations. The arena could not accommodate the onslaught of reporters; hence, the press stands were expanded from 120 to 420 seats. Pedro Salazar, PSV's Chilean media officer, said:

> *The team was the surprise of European football, and everybody wanted to know what was going on. Even a newspaper like* The Financial Times *was present. Of course, they had a business angle on the story. The whole world was watching. PSV was a phenomenon.*

People agreed that no matter how the semifinal against the Milanisti would end, the club could look back on a 'legendary season'.

In the end, PSV did not get the crown, but the media verdict was unanimous (including the Italian, astonishingly): the Dutch had the better team and got Milan on the run. *La Gazetta della Sporta*, the most authoritative sports daily of Italy, spoke of 'one of the most atrocious Milans of recent years'. The British *Guardian* thought that 'PSV's technique, attitude and team spirit were fantastic'. And the French *L'Equipe* said, 'Hiddink had the guts to show up with five offensive players and only two defenders against a highly gifted team that made their utmost effort to undo all football-playing.' The coach came up with a tactical plan that took the Italian side completely by surprise. No other team in the Champions League had been able to score three times against Milan. Still, a deficit of one goal on aggregate cancelled out the 3–1 PSV win. Sportsman Hiddink warmly embraced his flustered Milanese colleague Carlo Ancelotti at the dugout, and the 'atrocious' Italians went to the Istanbul final instead.

Hiddink concluded:

> *We put a world champion against the ropes with excellent, modern football. I am extremely proud of this team . . . The internal battle between pride and disappointment will last a little longer. Now the balance is tipped toward disappointment, but on Sunday we're going to celebrate and we will wash everything down with a good glass of beer.*

Even in Amsterdam's notorious red light district – one hundred per cent Ajax (the local pro-football club) territory – all TVs were tuned in to the game and praise was universal. The coach and the club received reactions from all over the world. Hiddink: 'From Hong Kong to Los Angeles, from Sweden to South America. People were profoundly impressed. Everybody agreed: This is how you play football.' He described his own feelings as 'calm and slightly numb' and tried to process the disappointment with a 'day in nature. I rode a mountain bike through the [southern Dutch] forests between Waalre and Valkenswaard. I also tried to play a few rounds of golf. But once on the course I noticed the tension still lodged in my body. I missed every ball.'

This feat was accompanied by a fifth national championship for the club under Hiddink. At the final match, he shed a tear. Very un-Hiddink-like, but maybe some of all that emotion had to find its way out after all. In addition, he provided PSV with its fourth Amstel Cup (the other coveted Dutch pro-football prize), out of the club total of eight. If numbers are the measure of things, then Hiddink must be considered the greatest Dutch coach of all times. He dethroned 'the father of Dutch football', Rinus Michels, who gave Ajax four national championships and three Cups.

When the dust settled, football aficionados wondered out loud: why on earth is Hiddink still in Eindhoven? His annual income at PSV has been estimated at 1.5 million euros (about A$2.4 million). That compares poorly to the 7.5 million of Mourinho, at Chelsea; the 6 million of Ferguson, at Manchester United; and the 5.8 of Eriksson, at the English federation, to name just a few. Meanwhile, Hiddink had been the money maker for PSV. UEFA paid the club 15.7 million euros – revenue from broadcasting rights and sponsor contracts. Not an enormous amount in football circles – champion Liverpool earned 30.6 million – but with a fourth place comes recognition and other income. Still, the coach himself has said on more than one occasion that it isn't all about the money. It's the game. And he's at home at PSV. He likes it there.

Hiddink is, more than anyone else, a reconstruction coach. He challenges the status quo. At Real Madrid, this method wasn't popular.

In Korea he made enemies through bypassing the old guard and pushing young players ahead. His selection was grudgingly accepted and the results astonished everyone, including himself. The great run for the Champions League was the same. Eighty per cent of the revamped team was recruited by Hiddink. The team that smoothly operated in the winter was 'a rough lump of clay' (Hiddink's words) in the creator's hands the autumn before. PSV was on a roll. Success feeds on itself.

PART VI

PREPARATION FOR WORLD CUP 2006

JUGGLING PSV AND AUSTRALIA

There has been no shortage of interest in the services of Guus Hiddink. PSV saw the possibilities, and the threats, early and pitched him for the position of club technical director. Head coach and technical manager in one – another first in Dutch football. Not everyone was enthusiastic about such a concentration of power – Hiddink would effectively shape the whole sports dimension of the club, solo. To put some cap on his authority, Jan Timmer, the chairman of the PSV board, insisted on an annual evaluation of the legislator-executive's performance. After some tedious negotiations, Hiddink signed a three-year deal and started to function in his new capacity from 1 July 2004.

However, Hiddink insisted that a clause should be included in the contract permitting him a role as World Cup coach of some national team 'on a project basis'. Soon after, the name China was floated. He was actually approached by the German football federation as a possible candidate to lead the national team. Imagine that. At a local press conference a camera crew of the German broadcaster RTL was prying. But all they heard from the reticent Dutchman was *kein Kommentar*, 'no comment', and as a goodbye, *gute Fahrt*, 'have a good trip'. Although Hiddink has indicated more than once in the past that he was 'tired of living out of a suitcase', his thirst for adventure, tension and acknowledgement has kept him looking for new springs. The back door of the world citizen from Varsseveld is always open. Maybe that was also what worried chairman Timmer.

In the condescending judgement of some Dutchmen, Hiddink became the 'part-time' coach of Australia. That's factually correct because he does divide his time between the Socceroos and PSV. But it is a misleading observation just the same because it suggests a partial commitment, and perhaps, a half-hearted investment. And that is not true. Hiddink's involvement in the management of both teams is total, and it shows. Not many of his colleagues would be capable of what he is doing right now. But in the Hiddink universe, the continental shifts from one side of the planet to the other seem relatively effortless.

Despite his cosmopolitan image, Hiddink is in for the long haul. PSV's 19 November game against RKC Waalwijk was a jubilee – his 250th match as PSV coach. He is only surpassed by PSV fixture Kees Rijvers, who coached PSV for 281 games, in the good old days. Under Hiddink's governance PSV has won 183 games, lost 25, and tied 41. Not a bad track record. So nobody in Eindhoven would like to see him go.

There is little cause for concern about an 'Australian distraction'. Only one player from the Australian team who was in the World Cup squad for the qualifier against Uruguay in Sydney played his football outside of Europe. That player was Archie Thompson, who at the time of the qualifier, was playing in the Hyundai A-League with Melbourne Victory. Archie has since been signed up by Guus Hiddink at PSV. So, Hiddink can comfortably set up shop in the north-west corner of Europe. And new PSV board chairman Rob Westerhof believes that Australia's glory and Hiddink's rising superstardom will positively reflect on his club and, hence, increase revenue. Pro-football *is* a business.

Hiddink did not come to Australia with the illusion that the Socceroos were among this year's World Cup best. But he got a good impression during his first brush with the players and decided that they compared rather favourably with the unpolished, internationally inexperienced, 'naïve' Korean squad he encountered in 2001. In his opinion, he did not have to 'start from scratch' as he had in Seoul. His later complaints about the team's shortcomings were, at least in part, self-serving – a vintage Hiddink device to exploit the media for his own purposes, to 'stimulate' his crew a bit. He needs to build the team spirit, sharpen the focus, instil that 'killer instinct' the boys lack and wake up the supporters.

HIDDINK AND THE SOCCEROOS

Hiddink came to Australia with the reputation of being a miracle worker. An earlier attempt to recruit international coaching talent to land an Australian berth in World Cup 1998 failed with Terry Venables, the former English manager. The disappointment was intense: Australia got knocked off the threshold to the tournament by Iran, who had drawn 2–2 in Melbourne, and had qualified on the away goal rule and that through an own goal. Hiddink has put balm on the old wound and his magic has worked so far. The Socceroos will be part of World Cup 2006, for the first time in thirty-two years and the second time in history. In some ways this will be a case of déjà vu. In 1974, the tournament was also held in Germany. That adds to the pressure to make the 'second coming' work better than the first. The 1974 Socceroos were all part-time players who sacrificed jobs and relationships in order to qualify and play in West Germany. They were playing against full-time professionals. The Socceroos lost 2–0 to East Germany, 3–0 to the 1974 World Cup champions West Germany and tied 0–0 with Chile in a game which was played in torrential rain, to earn Australia their first ever World Cup point. The 1974 Socceroos were pioneers for the game in Australia who performed admirably and won the respect of the German footballing public.

Unlike European or South American teams, the Socceroos never had the luxury of a gradual warm-up for World Cup qualification. In 2005, it was another two-time shot – first the Solomon Islands and then Uruguay. In the past, the Australians whipped the Pacific Island nation with a cumulative score of 12–1 before being defeated by teams such as Iran, Argentina and Uruguay. That would be equivalent to PSV playing a local amateur club and then getting knocked out of the Champions League by Arsenal or Manchester United. Not fair, really, and Australia were accepted into the Asian Football Federation on 1 January 2006. But at the time, the Socceroos were faced with another all-or-nothing scenario during the run-up to World Cup 2006.

Although the Solomon Islands are not known as a

football powerhouse, Hiddink did not take any risk during the encounters. He picked the strongest players from the selection: Mark Viduka (Middlesborough), Tony Vidmar (NEC-Nijmegen) and the attacking midfielder Jason Culina (FC Twente – like NEC, a Dutch club). Unfortunately, due to injuries, he had to do without attacker Harry Kewell (Liverpool) and former team captain Craig Moore (Newcastle).

The monster score of 7–0 in the home game was no reason for euphoria, at least not in Hiddink's opinion. 'Seven goals – that's not bad. I'm not unhappy with that. But against an opponent like Solomon Islands you owe it to yourself to win convincingly. There is room for improvement though. A Latin opponent is going to be an altogether different story.' The away game in Honiara with 2–1 sealed the islanders' fate, and Australia was guaranteed a visit to South America. On the three-and-a-half-hour flight back to Sydney, Hiddink was glued to a monitor, doing game analysis with his assistants Graham Arnold and Ron Smith, suggesting that his unease over the team's lack of preparedness to face a big gun was real. Once back at the training grounds of Lawson Tama Stadium – if it can be called that much in the absence of bleachers; the crowd squats on a grassy hill adjoining the pitch – Hiddink did not hide his misgivings over the practice performance and sent a chair flying from the dugout.

To gear up for the South American play-offs, he took the Socceroos to Holland, as he did with the Koreans before, for four days of training in the rustic surroundings of Hoenderloo and sports park De Ark in Mierlo. Because of its proximity to Eindhoven, Mierlo is a convenient location for Hiddink. The staff and regular clientele of the neighbouring hotel De Brug were not shocked – they are used to visiting football VIPs. The training sessions looked very much like an afternoon in Eindhoven. 'True,' said Hiddink, 'The approach is not much different from preparing PSV for the new season.'

During camp, the Australians were a picture of vigour and eagerness. Hiddink focused on developing tactical and strategic sensibilities, which in his view were much less prominent. 'We're going to get a tough opponent. Colombia, Paraguay, Chile or Uruguay. Chances are 60 to 40 in favour of the South Americans,' the coach coolly predicted. 'They play at the edge of the game. Australians don't really have that. Dedication aplenty – you can hardly get them off the field – but you also need shrewdness and a kind of mercilessness.' After camp, a friendly match against sparring partner Jamaica in London yielded a 5–0 victory.

Training sessions with Guus are no picnic – beefing up the physical endurance and mental toughness are the hallmarks of the regimen. With one two-and-a-half-hour practice session in the morning and one in the afternoon, players have little chance to stay soft. The proverbial relaxedness of the Australians was a bit too much for Hiddink. 'At the hotel, everybody ate whenever it suited them. That may be normal for them, but it isn't for us. So we sharpened things a bit. Because that kind of attitude will show on the field.'

AUSTRALIA–URUGUAY

There were some other reasons to be nervous about the away game in Montevideo as well. Four years earlier, the playoff between Australia and Uruguay turned into a football war. The visitors were cursed and spat upon by a small group of Uruguayans as they left the airport in Montevideo en route to the hotel. To avoid a replay of the imbroglio, John O'Neill, CEO of Football Federation Australia, and Hiddink decided to set up training camp across the Rio de la Plata in Argentina, near Buenos Aires. The 'hell of Uruguay' was to be kept to a minimum – no more than a 24-hour stay. The hosts interpreted this as a snub, a deliberate provocation, and an attempt to influence the referee and turn arbitration in Australia's favour. Some Uruguayan commentators proclaimed that Hiddink and his team were *maricones*, 'soft eggs', men not used to anything. At best, the Australian side was overreacting, was the verdict.

But Hiddink understands sports politics and is adept at turning a problem into an advantage. He also has a good grasp of how Latin American football works, and under no condition would allow the football sideshow – in this case the antics of the *hinchas*, the fans, supporters – to become a distraction. Meanwhile, he did not get too excited over the prospect of facing thousands of jeering people, considering it 'normal' to encounter hostility when you are in 'enemy' territory.

The arrival in Montevideo could have rivalled a visit from US President George Bush – not a popular figure in the south. At least 100 policemen were on hand at the airport, and the motorcade skipped all red traffic lights. Police chief Carlos Delpuerto informed the press that even for the Brazilian team he had not mobilised as many personnel. And that really means something in Latin America.

Two hours prior to the Saturday afternoon match, the Estadio Centenario was packed with 55,000 noisy Uruguayan fans. The 200 Australian supporters present were no match. Captain Paolo Montero announced before the game that his team would play with a knife between its teeth and the *hinchas* seemed to have picked up on the rah-rah. The entry of the Australian team was cause for a whistling concert and catcalls. The Socceroos responded with gentlemanly applause. While the Uruguayan national anthem played, two gigantic banners were unrolled in the stands, reading '1950' (the last time Uruguay was world champion) and 'History must repeat itself'. The message was clear.

The Australians started strongly, but after the only goal of the game by Uruguay, the result of a dubious free kick, the South American side dominated. At the end, the Australians sighed with relief and Uruguay supporters were visibly disappointed. 'Part-time' coach Hiddink confessed to having 'mixed feelings' about the outcome. In principle he was not disappointed with the score – the damage was limited – but felt that the Socceroos controlled the game and had partly dominated it. Under such circumstances it was 'a pity that you can't pick up a point. I'd rather have lost 2–1 than 1–0.'

In addition, the master saw more tactical shortcomings on his side. Some overeagerness to get into the opponents' box had the Socceroos go ballistic, quite literally, lobbing long-distance balls to the front, rather than giving a few smart short-range passes to build up the attack. 'We forgot to play our superiority in midfield. I think we gave it away, some dangerous situation,' reflected Hiddink later. Brawn over brain, in other words. His dissatisfaction was shared by his Uruguayan colleague Jorge Fossati, though for quite different reasons. Fossati apparently had decided that his team should have been starring in the game. But the attempt was unexpectedly frustrated. The Dutchman's influence paid notable dividends, and the Australians responded more maturely than in the past. Provocations that would have tripped up players until recently proved harmless. Before the match, Hiddink had exhorted his men to remain calm and 'patiently' force Uruguay to yield the spot in the 2006 tournament. To the people back home at PSV, such commentary rang familiar.

The heavy trip back to Australia, halfway around the world, was alleviated by the amenities on board the charter, generously provided by Qantas, a main sponsor of the FFA – beds, massage tables, exercise equipment, and even a jacuzzi. On board were two doctors, two physiotherapists and a masseuse. While the Socceroos enjoyed every comfort available, Uruguay was changing planes in Chile. In world-class football, everything counts. Hiddink did not expect that Uruguay would play an aggressive game in Sydney. 'But if they do anyway, my team knows what they are supposed to do. We know everything about our opponent and went over all possible options at the intensive training camp in the Netherlands earlier this month.'

Before the game started, Hiddink had asked for 'a very enthusiastic Australian crowd' to help pull the team across the finish line. It seemed like he was taking another leaf from the Korean book, where the 'twelfth player' had been instrumental in getting the reds as far as they did. But the appeal might have been superfluous – the supporters were out in force. The game in the boiling Sydney Telstra Stadium, packed to the rafters with 83,000 supporters, was intense. The Australians fought an uphill battle in the first half and were usually a man short in the exchanges. The South Americans had better control and better opportunities, particularly in Recoba, but missed.

Uruguay dominated in the first thirty minutes until Hiddink created order in the chaos by substituting a recovered Harry Kewell for Tony Popovic. Calm returned to the team, which culminated in a goal for Australia ten minutes before the break. The way the goal came about was somewhat illustrative of the general mood of the game. Kewell aimed at the goal from within the penalty area, but did not get his foot under the ball, which then landed well for Mark Bresciano, whose superb left-foot strike hit the top left corner of Uruguay's net, to finish the job off. The team played with passion – that key ingredient of world-class football so dear to Guus. Extra time was a nail-biter, as was the regulation time, but yielded no goals.

In the event of aggregate scores being tied, the outcome would have to be decided by penalties. Thinking that the home game might well end one goal in favour of the Socceroos, Hiddink had the team work hard on their penalty skills. He kept the curious guessing, saying that the technical staff would be making the final decision on who would be taking the shots. 'That list is already in my mind. But it also depends on the development of the game.' Apparently, the pressure build-up in the stadium during the second encounter with the Uruguayans was so overwhelming to some Australian supporters that they left before the fateful shootout took place. Allegedly, tearful fans escaped the scene of the presumed execution before the expected death knell was administered. Others doused the stress with liberal quantities of alcohol.

When the inevitable penalty period arrived, Hiddink could not field reserve Zeljko Kalac – former goalie of Dutch pro-club Roda JC now with Italian giants AC Milan, and Hiddink's preferred choice – because he ran out of options after having to field a third substitute, for injured Brett Emerton. Instead he had to rely on the man in position, Mark Schwarzer. This may have given Australia the ticket to Germany – we will never know for sure. The unanticipated set-back did not throw Hiddink off. He walked over to Schwarzer, spoke briefly with him, and they shared a laugh. Astonishing, considering the circumstances. It is a known fact that most penalty-takers shoot so hard that a goalie has to decide in advance which way the ball will go and dive in that direction. But Hiddink told Schwarzer that Uruguayans work differently. They wait for an instant to see which way the keeper heads and then tick the ball in the opposite corner. It is battle of wits. So Hiddink told Schwarzer to keep his cool and not dive early. It worked. Schwarzer made two saves, John Aloisi took the winning shot and the Hiddink legend ratcheted up another notch.

Immediately after the victory, when the stadium

exploded and players were beside themselves with joy, running around the field with their shirts pulled over their heads, the coach was standing alone for a moment in the centre of the pandemonium, his face impassive, the way we have seen him before, in Korea and elsewhere. Later, after relative calm had returned, he announced, 'I am going to thoroughly enjoy this with the boys for a bit; and then back to the Netherlands.' He characteristically included everyone in the success, 'not just the 13 or the 14 from today, but also the guys on the bench. We only worked together for four weeks. But they worked hard for it. It's a great team.'

International critics agreed: Australia was entitled to win. Not necessarily because they played superior football but because they wanted to win so badly and gave everything. Uruguay had the skill but not the sparkle. Heart won over technique. The management of the stadium sliced off the patch of turf from which Aloisi sealed the win, saying it would be freeze-dried, chemically treated, and encased in glass for future generations.

Prior to the game, star offensive player Alvaro Recoba, the 26-year-old leftie of Internazionale, ran over with self-confidence and declared that Uruguay had the 'god-ordained right' to go to Germany in 2006. No less. He also proclaimed that it was 'normal that a country as ours participates in the World Cup'. Rubbing it in still further, he added that Australia would have to wait at least another four years to participate in a World Cup. Pride has its deserts, the Dutch Reformed minister of Varsseveld would doubtless have observed, and in the end this boisterousness was punished, whether by God or by man is a matter of speculation. But for all practical purposes it seemed that the 'football gods' smiled on Australia. The Socceroos outran and outfoxed the opponents who outranked them by 37 spots on the table. As a result of the qualification, Australia was elevated six spots to 48th in the FIFA rankings, while Uruguay dropped a slot. Time for the Socceroos to gloat, at least temporarily.

The A$8 million committed to Australia by world governing body FIFA was a nice reward, for starters. With 30 per cent of the amount going to players, that meant roughly $100,000 in hand per person. But the Hiddink-engineered upset means more than just personal income. There is potential for the Australian sports scene to permanently change. Football may now go mainstream and secure a top spot alongside cricket, rugby and Australian Rules football.

After the Sydney victory and twenty-four hours in transit, Hiddink returned to the relative peace and calm of Brabant. At the 'welcome home reception' of three people there was little fanfare. Such are the Dutch. But Paul van Kemenade, the manager of the PSV training centre De Herdgang, had decked himself out as Crocodile Dundee for the occasion, or at least, so he thought – wearing a dashing green-yellow shirt and a straw hat, and clutching an inflated crocodile under his arm. Perhaps a forecast of what may happen to Dutch apparel if the Socceroos get far enough.

D'ARTAGNAN AND THREE (MORE) MUSKETEERS

Hiddink added another victory on his already stellar résumé, this time in the southern hemisphere. The Australian victory was not lost on PSV officials. Chairman Rob Westerhof predicted that 'people are going to pull at Guus left and right. I don't have a crystal ball and cannot foretell whether or not he is going to stay with PSV. But . . . we still have a Champions League to win!' Team captain Phillip Cocu thought that PSV would have to come up with some pretty strong incentives to keep Hiddink grounded in Brabant. 'His market value wasn't exactly bad to begin with . . . But he has once again shown what he is capable of. If Hiddink leaves, the loss for PSV would be considerable.'

His current hometown Eindhoven was likewise abuzz with speculation over whether 'PSV had become too small' for Hiddink. Nothing is certain in the world of football, and international interest in men of Hiddink's calibre is ever-present. That Hiddink was recently grilled for twenty hours by the judicial branch of the Dutch Internal Revenue Service over suspected tax fraud will do little to enhance his commitment to the Dutch football scene. The Dutch, unrelentingly preoccupied with egalitarian proprieties and cultivating a suffocating bureaucracy, have a way of chasing excellence abroad. The country may indeed be getting a little small for a man of Hiddink's stature.

This will be the third time in a row that Hiddink will be present at the World Cup – in 1998 with the Netherlands, in 2002 with Korea, and in 2006 with Australia. Meanwhile, Hiddink's colleague Leo Beenhakker led the Trinidad and Tobago team to a victory over Bahrain and brought the Caribbean island nation to its first World Cup ever. Trinidad and Tobago is only the fourth Caribbean country to make it to a World Cup – with Cuba (1938), Haiti (1974), and Jamaica (1998) the previous three. Dick Advocaat is trying to repeat the Hiddink feat with Korea, and Marco van Basten is bringing the Netherlands back to the World Cup after the embarrassing absence four years ago. That brings the grand total to four Dutch coaches at World Cup 2006, a historic national record. Brazil, Argentina and France each deliver three, and Sweden and Croatia two. 'Now we will be able to do some *klaverjassen* (a Dutch card game for four people in which the jack is a trump card),' joked Beenhakker after Trinidad and Tobago's decisive match.

In the meantime Hiddink continues to set the tone by executing his Socceroos–PSV juggling performance admirably. The southern Dutch club liked the taste of last year's Champions League streak and wants some more. They won all of their European level home matches without conceding a goal. Fenerbahçe was the last one to fall to the PSV axe, 2–0. Of all the most recent home matches, they won nine, with only giants Arsenal and Olympique Lyon getting away with draws. Now couldn't we have World Cup semifinals of Australia versus the Netherlands and Korea against Trinidad and Tobago? That would be delightful . . .'One for all, and all for one!'

WORLD CUP 2006

A television audience of 300 million people watched the World Cup draw in Leipzig, Germany. Australia got in a tough group. They face their first opponent, Japan, in Kaiserslautern on 12 June. Five days later they come out against World Cup favourites Brazil. The third team is Croatia. Hiddink was hopeful. 'Perhaps Japan and Croatia have other ideas, but realistically we are looking for the spot behind Brazil.' Japanese coach Zico called Australia under Hiddink 'highly motivated' and 'well guided'.

Nine million people watched the Socceroos defeat Uruguay on Australian television. It was one of the most watched television events of the decade. And the largest-ever global TV audience will watch the World Cup final next July in Berlin. That sounds promising indeed. It appears that 'Guus Geluk' is once again in the right place at the right time. But there is more to it than that. He places the players well, knows how to delegate responsibility, trusts, has things under control. He inspires confidence, keeps disturbances away from the team and helps players to manage the pressure. These are gifts not all coaches have.

Meanwhile, back home in the Netherlands, Guus' brother Hans, as always full of creative ideas and energy, has already conceived of various Varsseveld revival ideas. Perhaps inspired by the creations of the Bulgarian-American 'wrapping' artist Christo, he has proposed to pack up one of the ugliest buildings in the centre of town in an enormous cloth and paint it over in the brilliant orange colours of Uluru. In the local café, proprietor Jacques Westerhoff, a hulk of a man, paces the premises with a cell phone as a permanent fixture in his hand. He enthuses over the upcoming World Cup: 'Great! Samsung is in! Again one of those giant screens out front!' Hans Hiddink's band will perform a yet to be produced arrangement of 'Waltzing Matilda'. Bennie Joling of the extremely popular rock group Normaal, singing in Achterhoeks dialect, will join him for the occasion. Hans has also come up with a new name for the football teacher: *Kan-guru* (meaning in Dutch, 'Can-do guru'). Furthermore, Dame Edna will soon cut the ribbon at an all new Australian café in town, and kangaroos will be released in the Hiddink forest. If all goes as planned, this small town in the eastern Netherlands will soon be overrun by hordes of Australians, who have come to pay homage to their football saviour.

Of course, in professional football, things rarely go exactly as planned. And the sceptics, down under and up above, still think Australia is a long shot, and say they would be surprised if the Socceroos made it to the second round of the World Cup. But the believers, out west and back east, think that the ones who might actually be most surprised could be the Brazilians, who have the privilege of being grouped together with Australia in the first round. We have seen surprise outcomes before. The world is changing – China is facing down Germany economically, and India is tutoring America in online English. Even football is no longer monopolised by the old boys' club from Paris, Rome and Rio. That offers fascinating prospects for World Cup 2006. Especially when Guus Hiddink is in the running, third time straight, and with a group that wants to win as badly as the supercoach himself does. Look out! Here comes Australia with Guus Hiddink.

GUUS HIDDINK
CURRICULUM VITAE

Date of birth: 8 November 1946 in Varsseveld, the Netherlands

Schooling: Attended CIOS, Central Institute for Teachers of Physical Education in Overveen, 1965–1967

Career as player:

Varsseveld 1956–1967
De Graafschap, 1967–1970
PSV-Eindhoven, 1970–1971
De Graafschap 1971–1976
Washington Diplomats, USA, summer season 1976
San Jose Earthquakes, USA, summer season 1977
NEC-Nijmegen, 1977–1981
De Graafschap, 1981–1982

Career as coach:

De Graafschap, 1982–1984, assistant coach

PSV-Eindhoven, 1982–1984, assistant coach
PSV-Eindhoven, 1984–1986, assistant coach
PSV-Eindhoven, 1986–1990, head coach
Fenerbahçe, Turkey, 1990–1991
Valencia, Spain, 1991–1993; 1994–31 May, 1994
The Netherlands national team, 1 January 1995–12 July 1998
Real Madrid, Spain, 1998–February 1999
Real Betis, Spain, 2000–May 2000
South-Korea national team, 2000–2002
PSV-Eindhoven, 2002– present
Technical manager of PSV-Eindhoven, 2004–June 2006
Australian Socceroos, national team, July 2005–June 2006

Accomplishments as coach:
PSV-Eindhoven – five times national champion (1986–87, 1987–88, 1988–89, 2002–03, 2004–05); four times Amstel Cup winner; 1988 European (UEFA) Cup (now renamed Champions League); 2005 Champions League semifinals
The Netherlands national team – fourth place in the 1998 World Cup in France
South Korea national team – fourth place in the 2002 World Cup in South Korea and Japan

ACKNOWLEDGEMENTS

I would like express my gratitude to all the people who helped to make the creation of this book possible.

In the Netherlands: Friends and colleagues of Guus Hiddink allowed themselves to be interviewed and searched in archives and photo albums to find stories and pictures that helped to make the coach come alive on the pages of this book. The Hiddink family was kind and gracious in sharing anecdotes and thoughts about Guus. In particular, Guus' older brother Hans Hiddink was a great help. He was much more than a resourceful interviewee. He functioned as historian, local communications manager and Varsseveld tour guide. The good people of Hiddink's hometown, who have had to adjust so suddenly to overwhelming media attention, patiently responded to all questions and requests. Peter Verhagen, at PSV-Eindhoven, was resourceful and generously provided a choice selection of Hiddink photographs. Liesbeth Meijer, my sister, gave selflessly of her time and energy to keep the Dutch information supply lines running, long after I returned to Seoul.

In Korea: The people at Hyeonamsa Publishing managed to put out the original 2002 *Hiddink Biography* in a fantastically short period of time. My good friends Chris Johnson and Soonja Ahn provided not only an excellent Korean translation but were a wellspring of creative ideas. This foundation of the original was vital for the realisation of *Guus Hiddink: Going Dutch*. My wife, Myra, and my four children endured the long absences of their globetrotting, plane-hopping husband and father without complaint. They were a great source of encouragement and inspiration.

In Australia: Jamie Warren for his local knowledge of the Socceroos. Everyone at Random House, but in particular Jeanne Ryckmans and Chris Kunz, who did an excellent and efficient job of presenting a colourful and true-to-life Guus Hiddink down under.

ABOUT THE AUTHOR

Maarten Meijer spent his childhood years in a small town in the Netherlands. After completing his school education, he travelled extensively. When Europe became a little small, he sailed a yacht across the Atlantic Ocean to the Americas. After touring the Caribbean islands, he landed in the USA. He enrolled at the State University of New York, receiving a bachelor's degree in science and a master's degree in philosophy. In 1982, he met his wife, Myra.

In 1991, a taste for new adventure drove the family, which by then included a daughter and a son, to Russia. Maarten taught theology and philosophy in Moscow.

He received a PhD in Russian literature from Moscow State University, writing a dissertation on an old favourite, Leo Tolstoy. In Russia, the family befriended Russian Koreans and Korean natives and developed a taste for kimchi and Korean hospitality.

This ultimately inspired a move to Korea in 2000. Maarten taught English at a Seoul university for several years. Although he is fluent in English, German, Russian, Dutch and knows survival-French, he has not been quite as successful at mastering the Korean language, yet. He is the author of *What's So Good About Korea, Maarten*? and is currently writing a Dick Advocaat biography.

He now teaches at an international school in the Korean countryside, while continuing his activities as an author and social critic.

Maarten and Myra have a daughter and three sons.